DATE DUE			

Athlone French Poets

GÉRARD DE NERVAL

Athlone French Poets

General editor EILEEN LE BRETON
*Reader in French Language and Literature,
Bedford College, University of London*

MONOGRAPHS

Verlaine *by C. Chadwick*

Gérard de Nerval *by Norma Rinsler*

Saint-John Perse *by Roger Little*

CRITICAL EDITIONS

Paul Valéry: Charmes ou Poèmes
edited by Charles G. Whiting

Paul Verlaine: Sagesse
edited by C. Chadwick

Gérard de Nerval: Les Chimères
edited by Norma Rinsler

Saint-John Perse: Exil
edited by Roger Little

Gérard de Nerval

by

NORMA RINSLER

UNIVERSITY OF LONDON
THE ATHLONE PRESS
1973

Published by
THE ATHLONE PRESS
UNIVERSITY OF LONDON
at 4 Gower Street, London WCI

Distributed by
Tiptree Book Services Ltd
Tiptree, Essex

U.S.A. and Canada
Humanities Press Inc
New York

Printed in Great Britain by
The Garden City Press Limited
Letchworth, Hertfordshire
SG6 1JS

Athlone French Poets

General Editor EILEEN LE BRETON

This Series is designed to provide students and general readers both with Monographs on important nineteenth- and twentieth-century French poets and Critical Editions of representative works by these poets.

The Monographs aim at presenting the essential biographical facts while placing the poet in his social and intellectual context. They contain a detailed analysis of his poetical works and, where appropriate, a brief account of his other writings. His literary reputation is examined and his contribution to the development of French poetry is assessed, as is also his impact on other literatures. A selection of critical views and a bibliography are appended.

The Critical Editions contain a substantial introduction aimed at presenting each work against its historical background as well as studying its genre, structure, themes, style, etc. and highlighting its relevance for today. The text normally given is the complete text of the original edition. It is followed by full commentaries on the poems and annotation of the text, including variant readings when these are of real significance, and a select bibliography.

E. Le B.

CONTENTS

NOTE

All references to Nerval's works and correspondence are, except where otherwise indicated, to the edition in the Bibliothèque de la Pléiade, edited by Albert Béguin and Jean Richer, volume I (3rd edition, 1960) and volume II (1956). So as to avoid excessive numbers of footnotes, references to these volumes will be given in the text by title of work, volume number and page number: thus a quotation from *Sylvie* in the text will be followed by the reference (*Sylvie*; I, 241), or where the source has already been indicated, by volume and page number alone (I, 241).

The reference 'O.C.' followed by a volume number is to the *Œuvres Complémentaires* edited by Jean Richer (Minard, *Lettres modernes*); these volumes are listed in Section II of the Bibliography.

Reference to the Athlone Press edition of *Les Chimères* is indicated by L.C. in the notes.

FOREWORD

Since this volume is intended as a companion work to the Athlone Press edition of *Les Chimères*, I have devoted a good deal of space to an analysis of *Les Filles du Feu*, with which the sonnets were originally published, to *La Pandora*, which Nerval at one time intended to include in *Les Filles du Feu*, and to *Aurélia*, to which he refers in his introduction to that volume. In the section on the poetical works I have tried to show how Nerval's poetic gifts developed and culminated in *Les Chimères*, but the sonnets themselves are not studied here in detail. I am conscious that more might have been said, space permitting, about Nerval's writing for the theatre and about *Voyage en Orient*, both of which are discussed in general terms in the biographical section; some comment on the links between these works and the sonnets will be found in the edition of *Les Chimères*.

I would like to stress that I cannot claim to have produced a definitive 'interpretation' of Nerval's work, nor would I wish to do so. I would like the reader to look at the texts with a full awareness of the problems they raise, but with as few preconceptions as possible. In his life, we are told, Nerval was unfailingly modest and courteous. I believe that in his work he was not less anxious to treat his reader with respect, and that he meant to speak as plainly as his difficult subject would allow: it is we who have lost the gift of simplicity.

For Michael

I

GÉRARD DE NERVAL 1808-1855

The poet we know as Gérard de Nerval was born Gérard Labrunie, in Paris in the year 1808. Etienne Labrunie, his father, whose family came from the Midi, ran away from home at the age of sixteen to join the army of the Revolution. He was wounded in the left foot at Lille in 1792, and two years later his left leg was fractured. Discharged from the army, he became a student of medicine so that he could re-enlist as a military surgeon. In 1807 he married Marie-Antoinette-Marguerite Laurent, the daughter of a Paris draper, and less than a month after the birth of their child in May 1808, Dr Labrunie was attached to the Grande Armée, then in December to the army of the Rhine. Leaving her child behind, his wife travelled with him to Danzig and to Austria. In 1810 Etienne Labrunie was appointed director of the military hospital in Hanover, then of the hospital at Glogau on the Oder; in November, Nerval's mother died at the age of twenty-five, 'des fatigues de la guerre, d'une fièvre qu'elle gagna en traversant un pont chargé de cadavres' (*Promenades et Souvenirs*; I, 134–5); she was buried in the Polish Catholic cemetery at Gross-Glogau.[1]

The child, left in the care of a nurse at Loisy in the Valois almost since birth, now went to live with his mother's uncle, Antoine Boucher, in the nearby village of Mortefontaine. With no news of his father, the boy grew up a presumed orphan, affectionately cradled in the warm family life of his uncle's house. Forty years later he still remembered the Valois of his childhood as a lost paradise of innocence and happiness.

When the boy was seven years old, his father returned. He had been wounded a third time, at Wilna in 1812, and walked with a limp. Nerval describes (*Promenades et Souvenirs*; I, 135) how he was embraced so fiercely by the returning stranger that he cried out: 'Mon père! . . . tu me fais mal'. True or not, the account reveals the profound irruption his father made into Nerval's peaceful childhood. He seems to have been an essentially cold man, though like many such men he was sentimental: Nerval describes him weeping as he sang a song his wife had loved. Certainly he never established a close relationship with his son. Only a few months before his death, Nerval wrote sadly to his father: 'Si je mourais avant toi, j'aurais, au dernier moment, la pensée que, peut-être, tu ne m'as jamais bien connu' (20 June 1854; I, 1126).

At his father's home in Paris, Nerval's education was begun in earnest. 'J'étudiais à la fois l'italien, le grec et le latin, l'allemand, l'arabe et le persan', he tells us (*Promenades et Souvenirs*; I, 136). It sounds rather unlikely; but he certainly learned some German from his father, and he studied Latin, and some Greek, at school. In 1820, at the age of twelve, he was sent to the Lycée Charlemagne, where he rapidly made many life-long friends, of whom the closest was Théophile Gautier. The *lycées* had recently returned to the traditional curriculum based on classical literature, which the reforms of the Revolution had temporarily displaced. Some of Nerval's time was devoted to French history, philosophy and mathematics; but Greek and especially Latin authors occupied a very large place in his formal education. Not surprisingly, he preferred the poets to the historians; they remained an important influence, and their images reappear in his own mature work as symbols of his problematical self. Greece and Rome, with their art and their gods, were not dead, but still existed for him as a universal lost paradise which reflected his own.

Nerval was himself a precocious poet; his first poems were published in 1826, under the title of *Elégies Nationales*. But it was his translation of Goethe's *Faust* (Part I), begun in 1826 and published in 1828, which took him into the charmed circle of the literary *cénacles*, where he met Nodier and Hugo. It was not the first, but was considered the finest of the French translations of *Faust*, as Mirecourt recorded in 1854: 'c'est encore aujourd'hui la traduction la plus estimée que nous ayons de l'œuvre de Goethe'.[2] According to Eckermann, Goethe professed himself unable to read his own words any longer, but in Nerval's French version, he found the text new and fresh.[3]

In 1830, Nerval published *Choix de poésies allemandes*, his own translations from Klopstock, Herder, Bürger, Novalis, Goethe and Schiller, with an introductory essay. He certainly knew Mme de

Staël's influential work *De l'Allemagne* (1813), but his 'germanisme'[4] is not merely fashionable. Nerval had a deep sympathy for the German mind, and felt at home in Germany: 'Je t'avouerai que je sens mon genre d'esprit moins déplacé ici qu'ailleurs . . .', he wrote, 'Nous sommes tous un peu fous dans cette bonne Allemagne'.[5] He once referred to Germany as 'la vieille Allemagne, notre mère à tous' (*Lorely*; II, 743), and Germany was for him doubly a motherland, since it was the land in which his real mother had died. Among Nerval's unpublished notes there is a translation of a poem in which Heine expressed the same idea: the 'Pensées Nocturnes' ('Nachtgedenken'), in which Heine confesses:

> Nach Deutschland lechzt' ich nicht so sehr,
> Wenn nicht die Mutter dorten wär . . .[6]

But the influence of German literature on Nerval's work must not be exaggerated. The influence of his classical education was at least equally strong (he once referred to Greece also as 'notre vieille mère'). As Gautier remarked, Nerval, 'malgré son commerce assidu avec l'Allemagne et sa familiarité avec Goethe, restait beaucoup plus Français qu'aucun de nous; de race, de tempérament et d'esprit';[7] and Nerval himself noted: 'J'appartiens en littérature comme en pays à la tradition française' (I, 1211). In 1830 he had published, besides the *Poésies allemandes*, a *Choix des Poésies de Ronsard etc.*, with an introductory essay on the Pléiade.[8] In part at least the influence of Renaissance literature is that of a transmitted classical tradition; but other French influences are of equal importance: those, for instance, of the eighteenth century. His inheritance of the ideas of the 'philosophes' had a profound effect on him, indeed on all his generation, as he recognised. He was also interested in French history (cf. an early work, *Le Prince des Sots*, O.C. VI), and especially, like Hugo, in the history of Paris (cf. *La Main Enchantée*, 1832).[9] His love of folk-poetry links this aspect of his work with another: an abiding love of the French countryside, and especially of the Valois of his childhood, where, he felt, something remained of the noble simplicity his own generation had lost. The survival, in an alien world, of half-forgotten values and half-remembered beauties, is one of his most constant themes.

Despite his early taste of fame, life was by no means easy for Nerval. Dr Labrunie thoroughly disapproved of writing as a career. He was not amused by his son's unconventional friends— nor, one may suppose, by such incidents as Nerval's brief imprisonment 'pour tapage nocturne' in 1831, and again early in 1832, when he appears to have been involved in a political disturbance. Between 1828 and 1830 Nerval is thought to have been apprenticed to a printer and to have begun to study law. We know that he invented a printing machine, which was patented.[10] Eventually, in deference to his father's wishes, he became a student of medicine, continuing these studies until 1834, and assisting his father during the cholera epidemic of 1832. He was financially dependent on his father and in no position to argue; but he had not given up his intention of becoming a writer and continued to frequent the *cénacle* of the sculptor Jehan Duseigneur, and to cultivate the friends Dr Labrunie would not accept.[11]

In January 1834, Nerval's grandfather died, leaving him 30,000 francs, in those days a considerable sum of money. At the age of twenty-six, Nerval, who was still living in his father's house, suddenly found himself financially independent. Not surprisingly, the experience was an intoxicating one, and the next six years virtually constituted his intellectual and emotional adolescence. His first action was to leave at once for the South of France and Italy. He explored Provence, visited Florence, Rome and Naples, and returned by way of Marseilles and Nîmes, adding to his literary memories a stock of visual impressions of the Mediterranean landscape, so that this sunlit world henceforth embodied his dream of a golden age. On his return he set up house in an apartment in the Impasse du Doyenné, with Gautier, Arsène Houssaye, Camille Rogier the painter, and a fluctuating population of actresses, artists' models and other young writers and artists. It was his one period, after childhood, of almost perfect happiness: at least, so he said in 1853, looking back to these 'temps heureux': 'Nous étions jeunes, toujours gais, souvent riches . . .' (*Petits Châteaux de Bohême*; I, 66). In his article on Marilhat, Gautier offers us a brief glimpse of Nerval as a light-hearted companion:[12]

Gérard trouva un moyen de tout concilier, c'était de donner dans ce salon Pompadour un bal costumé . . .: cette opinion paradoxale nous surprit un peu, car nos finances étaient dans l'état le plus mélancolique; mais, poursuivit Gérard, les gens qui manquent du nécessaire doivent avoir le superflu, sans quoi ils ne posséderaient rien du tout, ce qui serait trop peu, même pour des poètes.

The eminently sociable Nerval was, however, the loneliest of artists. When he took part in the battle of *Hernani*, he was partly enjoying an adventure, partly offering his assistance to Hugo personally,[13] rather than defending or attacking any literary theory. His ideals inevitably show certain affinities with those of the Romantics, but they were not adopted because of his adherence to a group. The schoolboy Gérard had written: 'Unissons le noir Romantique / Avec le sévère Classique . . .',[14] and indeed, he always saw good on both sides of any question.

In May 1835 Nerval founded a theatrical journal, *Le Monde Dramatique*, in order, it is generally supposed, to celebrate the actress and singer Jenny Colon, with whom he is said to have fallen in love on his return from Italy. In fact the magazine devotes no more space to Jenny Colon in its lavishly illustrated columns than to others of the reigning theatrical beauties;[15] its attention may have furthered her career, but *Le Monde Dramatique* is not solely an advertisement of Jenny's charms and talent. Like other magazines of its kind, it preaches to the converted, ranging widely over the theatrical scene, past and present, French and foreign. Throughout 1831 and 1832 Nerval's literary interests had quite naturally centred on the theatre, where the Romantic movement was steadily extending its influence, and his founding of *Le Monde Dramatique* must be seen against this background. The venture was not a success: Nerval's legacy disappeared with astonishing rapidity, and worse, he was left, after the liquidation of his interests, with a burden of debt which was to harass him for the rest of his life. One imagines the comments of Dr Labrunie; but not less distressing was Nerval's own sense of failure and of guilt.

Nerval produced little work of substance in all this time, with the exception of *Piquillo*, written in 1836 in collaboration with Alexandre Dumas and the composer Monpou, and produced in 1837 with Jenny Colon singing the chief rôle of Silvia. In 1836

Nerval and Gautier signed a contract with Renduel for a work
to be entitled *Les Confessions galantes de deux gentilshommes périgour-
dins*. An advance payment allowed them to make a journey to
Belgium; but the work was never published, though their experiences provided copy for later individual writings (in Nerval's case
for *Lorely*, published in 1852). This pattern is repeated with
increasing frequency for the rest of Nerval's life; and his failure to
meet his contracts added to his sense of guilt.[16]

The simple necessity of earning a living determined henceforth
the pattern of Nerval's career, and his life-long interest in the
theatre must be attributed at least in part to this cause, for
success in the theatre meant immediate financial rewards, as well
as public recognition. More and more of his time was devoted to
journalism, and his serious literary work tended to be fragmented,
and often indeed was published as fragments to fill a vacant
column. We should not however dismiss his journalistic work, for
much of it is uncommonly graceful (the 'music criticism', which
consists largely of straight-faced summaries of outrageous opera
plots, is especially delightful),[17] and all of it displays, in varying
degree, his inimitable power of making every subject his own.
Indeed, the unguarded mood in which most of his *feuilletons* were
written allows us to detect his serious preoccupations, in some
respects, more easily here than in his formal writings. Patterns
were being formed in the poet's mind at this time which were to
become a constant condition of his thought. His poem 'Fantaisie'
(I, 18) expresses, as early as 1832, emotions which one recognises
as characteristically Nervalian; and Nerval himself acknowledged
their central relevance when he wrote, twenty years later: 'peu
d'entre nous arrivent à ce fameux château de briques et de pierre,
rêvé dans la jeunesse' (*Petits Châteaux de Bohême*; I, 75).

In the year 1832 appeared also his 'histoire macaronique', *La
Main de Gloire* (later re-titled *La Main Enchantée*), which indicates
an early interest in alchemy and the esoteric sciences. Esoterism
was a fashionable cult in the early years of the nineteenth
century, leaving its mark on the work of Balzac and others; and
as a journalist Nerval was always alive to the movements of
current opinion and belief: witness, for example, his penetrating
article 'Les Dieux inconnus' (1845; II, 1240–4). He too felt the
dissatisfactions of the time; but he also understood their nature

and their cause, and in an early manuscript[18] he notes the tendency of his generation to substitute for the God they could not accept, a variety of 'divinités mensongères'. Later, in *Sylvie* (I, 242), he described the spiritual unease which he and his contemporaries had experienced in their youth. The passage seems almost nostalgic for a time when the 'divinités mensongères' still seemed to offer some hope of salvation:

Nous vivions alors dans une époque étrange, comme celles qui d'ordinaire succèdent aux révolutions ou aux abaissements des grands règnes . . . un mélange d'activité, d'hésitation et de paresse, d'utopies brillantes, d'aspirations philosophiques ou religieuses, d'enthousiasmes vagues, mêlés de certains instincts de renaissance; d'ennui des discordes passées, d'espoirs incertains . . .

His personal salvation was not, in the event, to be mediated by magic alone, though he was ready to use in his work any strange or vivid detail, any hint of the mysterious or ineffable.

One of the 'divinités mensongères' of his youth appeared in the likeness of Balkis, Queen of Sheba: 'La reine de Saba, c'était bien celle, en effet, qui me préoccupait alors . . . Qu'elle était belle! non pas plus belle cependant qu'une autre reine du matin dont l'image tourmentait mes journées. Cette dernière réalisait vivante mon rêve idéal et divin' (*Petits Châteaux de Bohême*; I, 70–1). For this living dream, whose name was Jenny Colon, he proposed to write the libretto of an opera on the theme of her legendary rival. The opera was never written, but the material was later used in *Voyage en Orient*, where we may catch a glimpse of Nerval's shadowy ideal—of which Jenny was as much an image as Balkis herself, and no more real. Maxime Du Camp, who knew Nerval very well, rejects the idea that Nerval's unrequited love for Jenny Colon 'l'avait conduit d'abord à la ruine et ensuite à la folie', and comments: 'Ceci est une légende, et comme c'est Nerval lui-même qui l'a créée, il n'est pas surprenant qu'elle ait été adoptée et répétée par ses amis . . . La vérité est plus simple et l'on peut dire qu'elle est exclusivement pathologique'.[19] The legend continued to be adopted and repeated for many years to come; and it is not difficult to see why. Du Camp himself points out the alternative to its acceptance when he quotes Gautier's comment: 'Il a toujours été fou'. In other words, Nerval was mad indeed, but not with love. Du Camp reports a conversation between Jenny Colon and Gautier, in which she denied all knowledge of Nerval's passion for her.[20] We know that she was not invariably honest in her dealings with her lovers, but there was no reason for her to lie to Gautier—or Gautier to Du Camp; and Nerval himself says that the woman he loved 'ignorait jusqu'à mon existence' (*Octavie*; I, 290), and speaks of anonymous bouquets and unsigned notes (*Sylvie*; I, 269). Equally revealing is his reply to Gautier, who recounted Jenny's words to him: 'A quoi cela aurait-il servi qu'elle m'aimât?'[21] This can only mean that as far as Nerval was concerned, it was more important that he should be able to love Jenny, or the idea of Jenny, than that Jenny should love him. It is clear, indeed, that it would have been not merely pointless if Jenny had loved him, but actually embarrassing. He had no wish to come any closer: 'je craignais de troubler le miroir magique qui me renvoyait son image . . .' (*Sylvie*; I, 241). The choice of an actress is significant: a woman not one, but manifold, moving at a distance, bathed in the unnatural light of the theatre, beautiful, graceful and totally unreal. It seems likely that Jenny supplied Nerval with an essential element of his delayed adolescence: an image of womanhood to which he could attach the literary and idealistic notions of love that he had earlier lavished on the young girls of his Valois home. The poet tells us how the young men of his generation shunned real women and gave their loyalty to a dream: 'la femme réelle révoltait notre ingénuité; il fallait qu'elle apparût reine ou déesse, et surtout n'en pas approcher' (ibid.; I, 242).[22] The actresses of the Paris theatres were at this time the most accessible of goddesses for young writers, who generally wooed these capricious deities with rôles written to measure. Nerval's behaviour in this respect seems not to have been quite typical, for he was primarily interested neither in the chase nor in the capture. Like his own Fabio in *Corilla*, he preferred to worship his beloved from afar, rather than set about entertaining her in the flesh: 'il faudra être brillant, passionné, fou d'amour, monter ma conversation au ton de mon style, réaliser l'idéal que lui ont présenté mes lettres et mes vers . . . et c'est à quoi je ne me sens nulle chaleur et nulle énergie . . .' (*Corilla*; I, 309). That he was afraid of love is clear enough in many of his writings, but the tone of *Corilla* shows that he was capable of appreciating the humour of the situation as well as its melancholy, and it is unlikely that his attitude is entirely due to emotional difficulties. Nerval seems to have had a kind of indolence with regard to his physical existence in general: he enjoyed the good things that came his way, but rarely spent overmuch energy on seeking them out. It is known that the accounts of his love affairs in *Voyage en Orient* are largely—if not entirely—fictitious;[23] moreover he is singularly unsuccessful: Catarina has another lover, and la Vhahby a mysterious 'chasseur' and three children; Saléma, daughter of a Druse sheik, has a disapproving father—and as if religion were not sufficient barrier, fever intervenes. In *La Pandora*, the hapless narrator has to contend with a prince, and with the lady's bad temper. We are not very distant here from the realms of farce, as Nerval himself was aware. 'Hélas! mon ami, nous sommes de bien pâles don Juan', he admits (*Voyage en Orient*; II, 38).

It seems hardly likely, therefore, that Nerval would have made a serious attempt to capture the notoriously fickle affections of Jenny. Gautier denied that the *Lettres à Aurélia*[24] were actually addressed to Jenny Colon.[25] We shall presumably never know, but Nerval gave the title of 'Un Roman à Faire' to the letters published in *La Sylphide* (December 1842) after Jenny's death, and his title probably reveals the truth of the matter: whatever the man may have felt, it was not the lover but the artist in him who recorded the love affair. In the preface to his translations of Heine's poems, Nerval remarks: 'Qui ne voudrait souffrir ainsi? Ne rien sentir, voilà le supplice: c'est vivre encore que de regarder couler son sang' (O.C. I, 89). The 'regarder' implies a degree of detachment,[26] and indeed Nerval describes Heine's *Intermezzo* as 'l'analyse patiente et maladive d'un amour ordinaire sans contrastes et sans obstacles, et tirant de sa substance propre ce qui le rend douloureux ou fatal . . .' (O.C. I, 86). It has been suggested that Nerval's portrait of Heine is 'un auto-portrait de Nerval',[27] and there can be no doubt that the sympathy between the two poets was very profound. The *Lettres à Aurélia* can be seen as Nerval's own *Intermezzo*.[28] Both works offer a searching analysis of an unsuccessful relationship, dissected with a curious blend of lucid detachment and passionate concern—not merely biography, but an imaginative act. 'J'arrange volontiers ma vie

comme un roman . . .', Nerval admits in one of the letters (I, 758).
He seems, consciously or not, to have created the legend of Jenny
out of his urgent need to love, and the fact that she was unworthy
of his love made her doubly suitable for the part she had to play.
The real torments for him are not the infidelities or negligences
of his beloved—these he can rationalise, as he rationalised his
father's indifference. He feels the deepest anguish when his own
loyalty wavers, when doubts enter his mind, and he feels unable
to love: for that calls love itself in question, which is no less a
blasphemy than doubting God. Maxime Du Camp describes a
drawing by Nerval of 'une femme géante, nimbée de sept
étoiles . . . qui symbolise à la fois Diane, Sainte-Rosalie et Jenny
Colon'.[29] Goddess and saint are clearly much more than the
avatars of Jenny Colon. Rather one may deduce that they and
Jenny alike represented an important element of Nerval's
mythology. 'C'est une image que je poursuis, rien de plus', he
said (*Sylvie*; I, 243), and it is finally as an incarnation of the image
of woman that Jenny has for him her real significance.

In April 1838 Jenny Colon married the flautist Leplus. In
August Nerval went to Germany to join Alexandre Dumas in
collecting material for their projected drama *Léo Burckart*. The
play was accepted at the Théâtre de la Renaissance, but the
Government censor objected to it after interminable delays.
Nerval revised it completely in the following year, and this second
version was finally produced at the Porte-St-Martin in April
1839, when it was given twenty-six performances. This was a
respectable figure for its time, but the delays in production had
caused the theatre some financial loss, and *Léo Burckart* did not,
as Nerval had hoped, bring relief from his debts. Another play
written in collaboration with Dumas, *L'Alchimiste*, was produced
in the same month, but met with no greater financial success.
Jean Richer has been able to compare the published version of
Léo Burckart with the original manuscript.[30] The two versions
show interesting differences, notably in the emotional relation-
ships of the characters. It seems clear that at this time Nerval
himself was undergoing a period of emotional stress and
uncertainty.

Nerval's financial position was becoming very difficult and his
theatrical failure depressed him profoundly, as always. In the

autumn he set off for Vienna, where he was apparently entrusted with some kind of official mission, perhaps as a compensation for the censor's treatment of *Léo Burckart*. In Vienna he met the pianist Marie Pleyel, became friendly with Liszt, and wrote a series of articles on French literature for the Viennese newspapers. Beyond that, we know little of his activities. Typically, he wrote several accounts of this period, as of many others, in which events take on a different aspect according to the degree of emotional control that he can achieve. Gautier remarks that Nerval's aim in writing of himself was always to 'dérouter le lecteur'.[31] This is true, in general, only of his most intimate concerns; and if he prevaricated about the winter in Vienna, that in itself suggests that it was of crucial importance to him. It is generally assumed that he suffered humiliation at the hands of Marie Pleyel, though the nightmare experiences he recounts in *La Pandora* may not refer specifically to Marie Pleyel at all. Much more important, in my view, is the fact that it was in Vienna that Nerval was finally forced to realise the extent of his father's indifference. Writing rather diffidently to ask Dr Labrunie for a small loan to tide him over the first weeks, he was met with a blank refusal, and with severe criticism of his way of life, his profession, and his future projects. It was bad enough to be told that his plight was his own fault, and that the friends who had encouraged him in his foolishness had better save him from the consequences; it was worse to be told that he was wasting his time, since he evidently had no talent and would never succeed in making a living as a writer. Nerval's replies to his father are dignified and sad; but there is an oblique and bitter reference to this incident in *La Pandora*, where Nerval recounts how he hurried to the post office to see if his 'uncle' had sent him some money; through the envelope he can see that there is no money order inside: 'cette lettre insidieuse . . . ne contenait de toute évidence que des maximes de morale et des conseils d'économie' (I, 349). After Vienna, Nerval's view of his situation was radically changed. His adolescence was at an end, and his work now began to be centred around the great themes which he explored for the rest of his life.

In 1840 Nerval was responsible from May to October for the dramatic criticism in *La Presse*, replacing his friend Gautier who was travelling in Spain. In May and June he was also working at his translation of the Second Part of Goethe's *Faust*. In October he left for Belgium to attend the Brussels première of *Piquillo*, where, it appears, he met both Jenny Colon and Marie Pleyel again; he returned to Paris in a state of complete mental confusion, depressed and overworked, and in financial difficulties. In February 1841 his first obvious mental crisis overtook him.[32] Excited and hallucinated, he was taken to Mme de Saint-Marcel's 'maison de santé', and in March to Dr Esprit Blanche's clinic. His friends believed him incurably insane, and the critic Jules Janin published a flattering 'obituary' which Nerval did not at all appreciate.

In November he was restored to apparent health, and vigorously denied the charge of insanity: 'Je suis toujours et j'ai toujours été le même, et je m'étonne seulement que l'on m'ait trouvé *changé* pendant quelques jours du printemps dernier', he wrote to Mme Dumas (I, 904). It is true that he was in health and sickness the same person, subject to the same mood-changes and with the same preoccupations. But his situation had changed, for his literary reputation, his capacity for work and his plans for the future were apparently endangered by the threat of intermittent insanity.

About Nerval's activities in the year 1842 little is known. Apparently he continued to write his *feuilletons*. In June Jenny Colon died; and in December were published the letters known as 'Un Roman à Faire'. Since these were quite probably written earlier, Nerval seems to have produced little new work in this year. In December he left Paris for the East. He was to be away for just over a year: a long and arduous journey. He wanted to get away from Paris and the curious or pitying eyes of his friends; and he hoped to accomplish something that would re-establish his reputation. To his father he wrote: 'L'hiver dernier a été pour moi déplorable . . . Il fallait sortir de là par une grande entreprise qui effaçât le souvenir de tout cela et me donnât aux yeux des gens une physionomie nouvelle' (I, 909). The journey to the East was to be an absorbing and overwhelming experience. The definitive edition of *Voyage en Orient* appeared in 1851; but most of it was previously published as articles and short sketches in a bewildering multiplicity of journals, with the same passages serving many times. In 1850 the old scenario of *La Reine de Saba* found its place in *Les Nuits du Ramazan* under the title of *L'Histoire de Soliman et de la Reine du Matin*; in addition, the definitive version contained the account of the voyage to Vienna, which was made to appear continuous with the voyage to the East, and which had already been published in two separate journals in 1840–1. There is a suggestion here that other sources of inspiration had deserted him—a point generally stressed by bibliographers. But the fragmentary and protracted publication of this work also indicates his continued preoccupation with it; and there is no doubt that it grew during these years, and arrogated to itself more and more of his poetic substance. Nerval's *Voyage en Orient* is a major work of literature which has scarcely received its due measure of esteem. It is not a travel-book in the accepted sense of the term. The prosaic facts of Nerval's journey are probably best revealed in his rather disillusioned letters to Gautier: 'c'est l'Égypte que je regrette le plus d'avoir chassé de mon imagination, pour la loger tristement dans mes souvenirs' (I, 933). In *Voyage en Orient*, the poet's imagination comes into its own. Nerval as a traveller is unique in that he travels at once in space and in time, in a real world of humorous or dramatic incident and in an inner world compounded of literature, legend, memories and dreams. There is no question of confusion: he sees and records the real world as it is, at the same time as he relates it to the world of his imagination: 'c'est bien le soleil d'Orient et non le pâle soleil du lustre qui éclaire cette jolie ville de Syra, dont le premier aspect produit l'effet d'une décoration impossible. Je marche en pleine couleur locale, unique spectateur d'une scène étrange, où le passé renaît sous l'enveloppe du présent' (II, 84). He always preferred his imaginary world to coexist in this way with the real world, to be peopled by the living. It was not the dead past that concerned him, but the continuing tradition—hence his interest in legend and in folk-song. He thought of his own memory as a palimpsest, a manuscript on which one text has been inscribed over another (*Angélique*; I, 191): history, the memory of the human race, seemed to him also to consist of superposed layers of experience, like the successive layers of civilisation uncovered by archaeological exploration: the new did not replace the old, but was built on top of it. This notion is central to his conception of experience, and it underlies the theme of time in *Sylvie* and in *Les Chimères*.

Nerval's other work during this period included the series of studies which finally became *Les Illuminés* (1852); these were published at intervals from September 1839 until 1851. What chiefly links them is eccentricity; and indeed Nerval compares the work to an 'éloge de la folie'.[33] 'Quintus Aucler' offers some insight into Nerval's religious beliefs, and the study of Restif de la Bretone[34] is very much an *auto-portrait*, especially with regard to Nerval's conception of love. A similar preoccupation may be observed in his introductions to his translations of Heine's *Intermezzo* and *Nordsee*, published in the *Revue des Deux Mondes* in 1848, a work of luminous insight and beauty, and the culmination of a long collaboration with his friend Heine. The introductions are also extremely interesting for the light they throw on Nerval's ideas about the nature and scope of poetry,[35] and his own later poetry owes much to these reflections.

Between 1846 and 1848 Nerval was intermittently engaged on the opera *Les Monténégrins*, which was produced, with little success, in March 1849. An extravagant spectacle (now lost), written in collaboration with Méry and entitled *Paris à Pékin*, was banned, as it was considered to compete with the Opéra-Comique. These disappointments probably contributed to a second crisis, in this year of 1849; Nerval was in Dr Aussandon's clinic in April, and later with Dr Ley. His roman-feuilleton, *Le Marquis de Fayolle*, was interrupted and remained incomplete as a result. S. A. Rhodes has suggested that Nerval did not finish this novel because he could not, being too involved emotionally in the love story of Gabrielle and Georges.[36] There are other, deeper issues which Nerval tried to face in this novel, I think; they concern the relationship between the hero, Georges, and his parents, and were very probably connected with the mental disturbances of this year. In the following year (1850) yet another ill-advised theatrical project, *Le Chariot d'Enfant* (an adaptation of an Indian drama, again in collaboration with Méry), met with failure. Nerval, profoundly depressed, was again under the care of Dr Aussandon.

In 1851, with some collaboration from Méry, Nerval worked on his 'Faust'-play, *L'Imagier de Harlem*, which was produced in

December of that year;[37] he began also his translation of Kotzebue's *Misanthropie et Repentir* for his friend Arsène Houssaye (then director of the Théâtre Français). There are obvious links between *L'Imagier de Harlem* and the themes of *Aurélia* and 'Artémis', and it seems probable that Nerval was already conscious of the questions which these works endeavour to answer. He was certainly in a disturbed emotional state. In September he fell and hurt himself badly, apparently during a manic crisis, and probably spent some time at Dr Esprit Blanche's clinic in Passy. This mental disturbance was prolonged into 1852, with a further stay at the maison Dubois where he was treated for a 'fièvre chaude'. In May 1852 he went to Holland. In August *Lorely*, accounts of travels in Germany and the Low Countries, was published, and in November *Les Illuminés*. Both were composed chiefly of previously published work, with, in the case of *Lorely*, unpublished material of much earlier date. In October and November *l'Illustration* printed Nerval's *Les Nuits d'Octobre*, a wonderfully vivid account, realistic in detail and imaginative in concept, of his nocturnal wanderings in the city and the suburbs, of the night-dwellers he met, and of his dreams and visions. The imaginative realism of the first part moves almost imperceptibly into the matter-of-fact fantasy of the second, when the narrator has left Paris for the countryside around Ermenonville, which is also the background to *Sylvie*. This movement towards the world of dream and childhood is indicative of Nerval's development at this stage in his life. He describes it himself: 'Avec le temps, la passion des grands voyages s'éteint ... Le cercle se rétrécit de plus en plus, se rapprochant peu à peu du foyer' (*Les Nuits d'Octobre*; I, 79).

He was returning to his 'paradis perdu', travelling backwards in time and space to find not only a confirmation of his memories, but also the essence of his own nature, buried under years of disappointment and confusion. In 1846 he had begun a series of short journeys to the countryside around Paris; *Le Marquis de Fayolle* (1849) contains many oblique references to his childhood, and passages which prefigure *Sylvie*; in 1850 his work on *Les Faux-Saulniers* (part of which later became *Angélique* in *Les Filles du Feu*) had led him back to the scenes of his youth. *Les Illuminés* has for preface an evocation of his years in the Valois, 'La

Bibliothèque de mon Oncle'; in Restif de la Bretone ('Les Confidences de Nicolas') he particularly notes the vision of an idyllic past persisting in a wretched present, and of a country girl whose purity is opposed to a dangerous illusion. In spite of all his difficulties, the inspiration of these newly re-discovered treasures resulted in the pure beauty of *Sylvie*, published between two crises in 1853. In *Sylvie* we find again a magical fusion of fact and fantasy, an apparently limpid narrative which clothes a depth of mystery and confusion; that such a harmony could be struck from his inner discords indicates how firm a hand the conscious artist in Nerval still had.

The crisis of August 1853 had resulted in Nerval's removal to Passy, where the clinic was now directed by Dr Émile Blanche. In December Alexandre Dumas, without consulting Nerval, published the sonnet 'El Desdichado', together with some references to Nerval's mental condition which the poet greatly resented. As in 1841, he felt that his good name was at stake; but he could no longer feel that time was on his side. He set to work feverishly to consolidate his reputation by means of a definitive edition of his works: in 1853–4 he published successively *Petits Châteaux de Bohême*, *Contes et Facéties*, and *Les Filles du Feu* together with *Les Chimères*.

In 1854 he left Passy for a final confused, despairing and exalted voyage to Germany. Jean Richer has conjectured that while he was in Leipzig, Nerval may have gone to visit his mother's grave at Glogau. His letters reveal that excessive elation at the beginning of his journey was rapidly replaced by profound depression. He was much disturbed by the publication of Mirecourt's monograph *Gérard de Nerval*,[39] and seems to have regarded it as a kind of posthumous tribute, like the premature obituaries written by Janin in 1841 and Dumas in 1853—in a letter to Georges Bell[40] he calls it a 'biographie nécrologique' (I, 1115). On his return from Germany he was obliged to seek refuge once more at Passy. Here he worked at his last book, *Aurélia*,[41] whose creation was attended by the most agonising difficulties of expression.

In October Nerval recovered his freedom of movement, against his doctor's advice, by appealing to the Société des Gens de Lettres.[42] He continued to work at *Aurélia*, and letters written at this time show that publication of the first part was several times delayed while Nerval corrected and added to the text. It was of overwhelming importance to him, and he was obsessively anxious to get it right. In December *l'Illustration* began the publication (which extended until February 1855) of *Promenades et Souvenirs*, in which many of the themes and backgrounds of *Sylvie* reappear. In *Promenades et Souvenirs* however the tone is more frankly confessional, and more sad. Nerval attempts in this work to consider the events of his childhood dispassionately, and for the first time refers directly to his family. There is a melancholy sense of an ending about these pages: 'le monde est désert' (I, 139); the past which he had evoked in *Sylvie* as a warm and living body, appears in *Promenades et Souvenirs* as a tragic ghost, and the whole work is haunted by a sense of homelessness.

Nerval remained homeless for the last few weeks of his life. The liberty he had fought for was to prove fatal. He wandered from one temporary shelter to another, disappearing from sight of his anxious friends for days at a time. The first part of *Aurélia* appeared in the *Revue de Paris* on 1 January 1855. On 23 January he gave to Paul Lacroix a carefully-made list of his complete works: a last pathetic gesture towards literary respectability. At dawn on the 26th he was found hanging in the rue de la Vieille-Lanterne.

Dr Blanche had no doubt that Nerval had killed himself 'dans un accès de folie' (I, 1170). His friends tried to save him from the stigma of suicide, and to ensure a Christian burial for him, by suggesting that he had been attacked; his assassins, they claimed, were the ruffians among whom Nerval had often wandered, and who no doubt mistook him for a police spy. It has also been suggested that the poet was hanged by accident. About this lonely death, as about his life, the legends have grown. We may reasonably assume that depression and the frost finally decided the wavering mind to release itself from its seemingly pointless sufferings. What matters to us, as to Nerval himself, is the work that was born of those sufferings.

THE TRANSFORMATION OF EXPERIENCE

The various literary influences which we have noted in Nerval's writings clearly do not alone explain the characteristic quality of his work. Nerval was not a chameleon; he was a man of firmly individual character who changed the things he touched rather more than those things changed him. It is often suggested that what we can discover about the personality of an artist tells us nothing about his art. This may be true in some measure of some writers; but Nerval himself stated quite clearly that there was a close connection between his life and his work (*Promenades et Souvenirs*; I, 139): 'je suis du nombre des écrivains dont la vie tient intimement aux ouvrages qui les ont fait connaître'. The statement is characteristically ambiguous: does it mean that the works are derived from his life, or his life from the works? The latter suggestion is not so strange as it may sound: he also said 'J'arrange volontiers ma vie comme un roman' (I, 758). In either case, it is clear that he thought the two inseparable, so that some knowledge of his life and of his personality should help the reader to approach his work.

We are fortunate in possessing photographs of Nerval.[1] They were made by Nadar (Félix Tournachon) in 1854, the year before Nerval's death; the poet was then in his forties, but the impression is of a man considerably older. He sits upright in his chair, his hands held self-consciously in his lap, and seems a little diffident about being photographed. Gautier's description of his friend gives us a glimpse of the poet in movement: he was quick, light, and graceful: 'il était tout ailes, et n'avait pas de pieds'.[2] Champfleury noted that 'Il y avait dans la physionomie de Gérard quelque chose de bienveillant',[3] and this benevolence was not merely superficial. His sociability and good nature have been attested by all those who knew him well. Gautier says: 'Cette bonté rayonnait de lui comme d'un corps naturellement lumin-eux . . .',[4] and Heine remarks that Nerval had no enemies; he describes his friend's goodness in the preface to *Poëmes et Légendes*, which included the translations on which Nerval and he had worked together:[5]

rien de l'égoïsme artiste ne se trouvait en lui; il était tout candeur enfantine; il était d'une délicatesse de sensitive; il était bon, il aimait tout le monde; il ne jalousait personne; il n'a jamais égratigné une mouche; il haussait les épaules quand, par hasard, un roquet l'avait mordu.

Nerval for his part was troubled by Heine's quick temper and ruthless judgement: 'C'est là l'ombre de sa lumière' (O.C. I, 85).

Nerval was a loyal friend, and more concerned with manifesting his feelings for his friends than with ascertaining their feelings for himself. That he was aware of this distinction is evident from a remark in one of his notebooks (I, 428): 'J'ai toujours distingué deux sortes d'amis: ceux qui exigent des preuves et ceux qui n'en exigent pas.—Les uns m'aiment pour moi-même et les autres pour eux'. Gautier notes that Nerval was always ready to do whatever he could to help his friends, and adds perceptively: 'il semblait vraiment qu'on obligeât Gérard en lui demandant service, il vous remerciait presque d'avoir songé à lui . . .'[6] To love others, to give affection and attention, was a necessity for Nerval. In his account (*Voyage en Orient*; II, 350–1) of his meeting with Saléma, he tells us how overjoyed he was to be able to feel his growing passion and watch over it 'comme une proie dans la solitude'; and when, in *Aurélia*, he speaks of his feelings for the woman he met in Vienna, he frankly admits the prior importance of his own ability to love (I, 360): 'J'étais si heureux de sentir mon cœur capable d'un amour nouveau! . . .' The same consideration, as we have seen, governed his attitude to Jenny Colon. This is perhaps the most important factor in the barrier which arose between Nerval and his father, and at the same time it explains Nerval's perseverance in seeking Dr Labrunie's approval. Symbolic of their unhappy situation is an incident in *Aurélia* (I, 396): 'J'allai visiter mon père, dont la servante était malade, et qui paraissait avoir de l'humeur. Il voulut aller seul chercher du bois à son grenier, et je ne pus lui rendre que le service de lui tendre une bûche dont il avait besoin. Je sortis consterné'. Misunderstanding was obviously inevitable, for the father was temperamentally incapable of accepting those proofs of affection which his son needed to give.

Nerval's attentiveness to others shows itself in the immediacy of his impressions of the world. Modern criticism of Nerval has tended to stress his 'dreamlike' or 'mysterious' aspects, and it is often forgotten that he was an exemplary realist. His landscapes are alive with minutely observed detail, noted with loving care by one whose interest lies in living, breathing things: hence his disappointment at the temples of Herculanum: 'Il fallait que cela fût peuplé de figures vivantes' (*Octavie*; I, 291); and hence his decision not to visit the ruined city of Thebes: 'Les mœurs des villes vivantes sont plus curieuses à observer que les restes des cités mortes . . .' (Letter to his father; I, 920). His observation, moreover, was never cool or detached, but essentially sympathetic. Nor was he deceived by the surface appearance. He recognised the brutality beneath the glitter of Vienna, and in Cairo he saw not the fabled Orient but an accumulation of human dwellings, dusty, decrepit and rather saddening (*Voyage en Orient;* II, 40, 96). His descriptions of people especially show the warmth of his nature: his observation is at once realistic and affectionate. His soldiers, travellers, policemen, magistrates, peasants and Parisians are not types, but individuals, and one recognises their humanity immediately. Nerval's realism is of the purest kind, devoid of the romantic disgust with life which lies behind much nineteenth-century 'realism'. There are the beautifully observed soldiers in *Promenades et Souvenirs* (I, 132), with their authentic voice and wayward reasoning; and the rapid sketches of *Les Nuits d'Octobre*: the young man listening to the advice of 'l'imposante matrone', the woman who had been 'une des *merveilleuses* de ce temps-là', and the philosopher of divine and human law (I, 93, 101–2). Of these last two characters Nerval remarks: 'Si tous ces détails n'étaient exacts, et si je ne cherchais ici à daguerréotyper la vérité, que de ressources romanesques me fourniraient ces deux types du malheur et de l'abrutissement!' (I, 102). He saw directly and clearly: there is no trace of sentimentality or of that mystique of the 'common man' which implies inevitably that the common man is being viewed from a distance. Nor is he inclined to reforming zeal, which equally requires a degree of detachment. In Nerval's play *Léo Burckart*, says Gautier, we find 'nulle colère, nul emportement, pas une tirade déclamatoire, mais partout une raison claire et sereine, une indulgence pleine de pitié et de compréhension'.[7] In his attempt to 'daguerréotyper la vérité', Nerval explicitly disclaims any social or political aims: 'Un simple écrivain ne peut que mettre le doigt sur ces plaies, sans prétendre à les fermer' (I, 102). He was unable to dissociate himself from the life he observed and put himself in the position of a manipulator of men. His view of the world is often humorous (and it is easy to forget that the poet of *Les Chimères* had a lively sense of humour) but never truly satirical. In his article on Heine, Nerval himself stresses the difference between affectionate laughter and the wit of certain satirists, 'esprits secs, haineux, d'une lucidité impitoyable, qui ont manié l'ironie, cette hache luisante et glacée, avec l'adresse froide et l'impassibilité joviale du bourreau' (O.C. I, 73–4). Such cold detachment was foreign to his nature. Alfred Meissner describes him as 'ein weiches, zartes Gemüt' and Schmidt-Weissenfels speaks of 'sein weiches, melancholisches Gemüt'.[8] There was evidently something soft and gentle in him which held him back from excess: Du Camp notes 'des allures humbles et penchées qu'égayait souvent un rire sonore et qui ne l'empêchaient pas d'aimer les discussions un peu vives', and adds: 'On l'aimait car son caractère était d'une aménité touchante'.[9]

He was in every way a tactful and undemanding man, and deliberately self-effacing: witness his habit of using pseudonyms. 'Son nom prononcé le faisait subitement disparaître', says Gautier, adding that in an age when flamboyant costume was the rule, 'Gérard s'habillait de la façon la plus simple, la plus invisible pour ainsi dire'.[10] Such ambition as he had was due primarily to his wish to justify himself in the eyes of his father; and his personal modesty is matched by his evaluation of the importance of his work. He never claims superiority by reason of his gifts, and regards his profession as no more (but no less) important than any other. He was concerned to see that writers, who in his time could no longer depend on the patronage of the rich, and whose freedom of expression could be threatened by acceptance of a Government pension, should not be cheated of the material rewards which they had earned. He believed that an author's legal and social rights should be safeguarded;[11] but he claimed no unearned privileges, and seems always to have regarded his work as the return he owed to society, to his friends, to his father, to life itself perhaps (Letter to Dr Labrunie; I, 1110):

je dois à la confiance des personnes qui m'ont soutenu de faire quelque chose de bon, peut-être d'utile . . . Mes ouvrages sont un capital que j'augmenterai, s'il plaît à Dieu, et qui, fût-ce après la mort, suffirait à m'acquitter envers les hommes.

There is an obvious link between this attitude and the feelings of guilty indebtedness which Nerval expresses in his madness: 'Il y a quelque chose que je n'ai point payé par ici . . .' (*Aurélia*; I, 400). Indeed, all the basic traits we have considered are constantly evident in Nerval's character; but his reactions and behaviour were profoundly influenced by the fluctuating moods to which he was subject. His conscientiousness, for instance, shows itself as diligence and moral seriousness when his mood is equable: he speaks of 'cette obstination lente qui m'est naturelle' (*Angélique*; I, 179). But when he is depressed, it becomes a painful obsessiveness: in a letter to his father (I, 1067), he describes his feelings of despair in 1853, during his enforced inactivity in the Maison Blanche, as 'une irritation qui ne tenait qu'à la crainte de ne pouvoir faire mes affaires et répondre à mes engagements'. Anxiety about small debts unpaid, or apologies due for minor offences, often recurs in his letters and haunts *Aurélia*: 'La masse des réparations à faire m'écrasait en raison de mon impuissance' (I, 395). In his elated moods he shows the imprudence in the conduct of business affairs, due chiefly to over-optimism, which is common in men of his temperament; one may observe the same phenomenon in the case of Balzac, and it is said indeed that it was Balzac who suggested to Nerval that he should found a review.[12] When his enterprises failed, Nerval's optimism deserted him at once; he became depressed and unhappy, unable to see any solution to his problems, which all seemed to conspire together to afflict him: 'Des difficultés surgirent' he says; 'des événements inexplicables pour moi semblèrent se réunir pour contrarier ma bonne résolution . . .' (*Aurélia*; I, 395–6).

The alternation of his moods was not of course dependent only on external circumstances. It was due to an inborn disposition which determined also the nature of his madness. This question is of some importance, for it has a direct bearing on certain characteristics of his work. His own testimony, and that of those who knew him, reveals a life-long pattern of alternating moods, varying normally between elation and mildly depressed inertia,

* *

and swinging more violently in times of crisis between a manic state and a state of severe depression. Nerval describes this pattern himself in his sonnet 'Épitaphe' (I, 44):

> Il a vécu tantôt gai comme un sansonnet,
> Tour à tour amoureux insoucieux et tendre,
> Tantôt sombre et rêveur comme un triste Clitandre . . .

and again in *Voyage en Orient*: 'Il y a des moments où la vie multiplie ses pulsations en dépit des lois du temps, comme une horloge folle dont la chaîne est brisée; d'autres où tout se traîne en sensations inappréciables ou peu dignes d'être notées' (II, 425). His friend Maxime Du Camp says: 'Ses accès, qui tantôt le déprimaient jusqu'au coma et tantôt le surexcitaient jusqu'à la fureur, ne duraient guère plus de six mois; il en sortait lentement comme un homme mal éveillé qui est encore sous l'impression du rêve'.[13] Kretschmer traces this pattern in the life of Goethe,[14] and it is equally evident in Goethe's translator. Periods of intense, almost feverish activity alternate with profound depression and inability to work. With advancing age, the brighter moods are briefer and less truly established, while the depressions become more severe. The delicate balance may be disturbed, and the mood-changes become more violent and more extreme. But it is important to realise that Nerval did not suddenly 'go mad', and it would be mistaken to look for any single immediate cause of the great crises in his life. The basic personality remains consistent throughout: in youth, a swinging between gaiety and melancholy; in middle age, between exaltation and despair. Nerval himself was aware that this was so: hence his stout denial, after the crisis of 1841, that he was 'changé'.

Nerval's manic flights did not alarm him, and though he later came to recognise the necessity of dissimulating, he was always inclined to think of them as 'privileged moments', and to defend himself against the charge of abnormality (*Aurélia*; I, 359):

je ne sais pourquoi je me sers de ce terme maladie, car jamais, quant à ce qui est de moi-même, je ne me suis senti mieux portant. Parfois, je croyais ma force et mon activité doublées; il me semblait tout savoir, tout comprendre; l'imagination m'apportait des délices infinies. En recouvrant ce que les hommes appellent la raison, faudra-t-il regretter de les avoir perdues? . . .

He believed that his mind, in his manic moods, underwent not a change, but an astonishing increase in power. On his release from Passy in 1841, he wrote to Mme Ida Dumas (I, 904):

Je suis toujours et j'ai toujours été le même . . . mais comme il y a ici des médecins et des commissaires qui veillent à ce qu'on n'étende pas le champ de la poésie au dépens de la voie publique, on ne m'a laissé sortir et vaguer définitivement parmi les gens raisonnables que lorsque je suis convenu bien formellement d'avoir été *malade*, ce qui coûtait beaucoup à mon amour-propre et même à ma véracité.

The confidence he expresses here did not last long; indeed in the same letter he confesses: 'je me trouve tout désorienté et tout confus en retombant du ciel où je marchais de plain pied, il y a quelques mois'. He was soon at the opposite pole of depression.

His depressions, to a varying extent, cut him off from the world around him (*Aurélia*; I, 394):

Les visions qui s'étaient succédé pendant mon sommeil m'avaient réduit à un tel désespoir, que je pouvais à peine parler; la société de mes amis ne m'inspirait qu'une distraction vague; mon esprit, entièrement occupé de ces illusions, se refusait à la moindre conception différente; je ne pouvais lire et comprendre dix lignes de suite. Je me disais des plus belles choses: 'Qu'importe! cela n'existe pas pour moi'.

He becomes anxious, shy and secretive, feels inferior and guilty, and shuns the company of others. 'Ne comptez pas sur moi pour une réunion de fête. Je souffre trop—moralement je veux dire', he writes to Dr Blanche in 1854 (I, 1143). To Méry he is more explicit: 'Je n'aime plus à me rencontrer avec vous . . . parce que vous me consolez'.[15] As he wrote to his father in 1842 (I, 909): 'le sentiment de ne pouvoir exciter que la pitié à la suite de ma terrible maladie m'ôtait même le plaisir de la société'. He suspects that he is being victimised, as he hints darkly in a letter to his father from Passy in 1853 (I, 1063): 'L'agitation nerveuse, je ne puis la nier, mais qui en est la cause? . . . nous vivons dans une époque de complots et je me méfie de tous, excepté de ceux que je sens bienveillans. Ils sont rares.' He had expressed similar suspicions during his first crisis, in a letter to Edmond Leclerc: 'j'ai cru saisir dans bien des choses qui me sont arrivées tant à Paris qu'à Vienne et à Bruxelles une certaine intrigue ou du moins un certain jeu convenu dont je ne possède pas l'intelligence complète' (I, 887). Again, he suspects some unknown agency to be instrumental in defeating his attempts to gain the confidence of Aurélia: 'Je ne sais; il y a des obstacles que je touche sans les voir, des ennemis que j'aurais besoin de connaître' (*Lettres à Jenny Colon*; I, 750–1). This suspicion of others seems in part to be a reflection of his own uncertainty as to whether he was inspired by good or evil, or was perhaps inhabited by both 'le bon et le mauvais génie' (*Aurélia*; I, 381). As his insight into his illness grew, these feelings were accompanied by despair, because he knew them to be unjust but could not control them. This in turn increased his feeling that there was some evil in him. Maxime Du Camp remarks perceptively of Nerval's behaviour in 1854: 'Lui, si doux, si enfantin d'habitude, il avait des accès de méchanceté, il les prévoyait et sentait qu'il n'était plus le maître de les dompter'.[16] This is the mood he describes himself, at about the same period, in his poem 'Madame et Souveraine', addressed to Mme de Solms (I, 43):

> Méfiant comme un rat, trompé par trop de gens,
> Ne croyant nullement aux amitiés sincères,
> J'ai mis exprès à bout les nobles sentiments
> Qui vois poussaient, madame, à calmer les tourments
> D'une âme abandonnée au pays des misères.
> Daignez me pardonner cet essai maladroit . . .

Afterwards he was always bitterly ashamed: 'J'ai eu tort, sans doute, de n'avoir pas eu plus de confiance; mais l'inquiétude m'a fait passer des jours et des nuits terribles . . .'; 'Rien ne m'attriste comme de penser que vous pourriez m'en vouloir encore de l'irritation maladive que j'avais conservée, sortant de chez vous . . .' (Letters to Dr Blanche; I, 1145, 1167).

Depression not only affected his view of the present, but also cast a retrospective shadow over his earlier life (*Aurélia*; I, 393):

Le sentiment qui résulta pour moi de ces visions et des réflexions qu'elles amenaient pendant mes heures de solitude était si triste, que je me sentais comme perdu. Toutes les actions de ma vie m'apparaissaient sous leur côté le plus défavorable, et dans l'espèce d'examen de conscience auquel je me livrais, la mémoire me représentait les faits les plus anciens avec une netteté singulière.

Remorse for past actions can paralyse the will, and it effectively prevented him from making the decisions which might have freed him from depression. He could only wait for a sign that his mood was changing.

Though his manic flights were damaging to his reputation, the real danger lay in Nerval's periods of depression. It is greatly significant that in the letter to Mme Dumas already cited above (p. 24), he links his supposed madness (that is, his manic elation) with 'le champ de la poésie'. Conversely, his accounts of his depressions show that their chief characteristic is a feeling of impotence and sterility, of inability to create. 'L'hiver dernier a été pour moi déplorable, l'abattement m'ôtait les forces, l'ennui du peu que je faisais me gagnait de plus en plus', he wrote to his father after the first crisis (I, 909). The same despair is evident in a letter to Victorien Mars written on the eve of the crisis of 1853: 'Je n'arrive pas. C'est déplorable. Cela tient peut-être à vouloir trop bien faire . . . Je vais toujours néanmoins, si je puis aller, car ce n'est pas maladie réelle, mais lourdeur d'esprit . . .' (I, 1041). 'Vous savez,' he explains to Georges Bell, 'que l'in-quiétude sur mes facultés créatrices était mon plus grand sujet d'abattement' (I, 1131). This haunting fear of sterility is surely, for an artist, the worst of all. Almost the last recorded words of Nerval reflect it clearly: 'Je ne sais ce qui va m'arriver . . . mais je suis inquiet. Depuis plusieurs jours je ne puis littéralement plus écrire une ligne. Je crains de ne pouvoir plus rien produire . . .'[17] The next morning he was found dead.

By 'vouloir trop bien faire' Nerval did not mean mere polishing of style. His meticulous correction and revision of his manuscripts, and of the proofs, bear witness to his desire for 'une édition classique et pure de fautes autant que possible' (Letter to G. Charpentier; I, 1004); but his letters show that the corrections were always designed primarily to improve the clarity of the text: 'j'ai un petit changement à faire pour éclaircir le dénouement', he writes to Giraud (I, 1084), and the theme is taken up again and again in his letters to his publishers and printers; his desire for accuracy even led him, he told Charpentier, to submit a passage to 'des gens de Constantinople pour éviter les inexactitudes'— one is reminded of Balzac writing to Mme Carraud to check the names of some streets in Angoulême.[18] This type of correction, similar to those which he made to his poems, shows a primary interest in the content of his writing. It is of course largely illusory to consider art as split into 'form' and 'content', since neither is viable alone. The fact remains that artists themselves will often emphasise one aspect rather than the other. Nerval appreciated the necessity for formal conventions in art: 'L'art a toujours besoin d'une forme absolue et précise, au delà de laquelle tout est trouble et confusion', he writes in the 1840 introduction to his translation of *Faust* (O.C. I, 13); but he considered the form of a work of art to be subordinate to its content. He endorses the opinion of Goethe, which he quotes with evident approval (again in the 1840 introduction to *Faust*), and which he describes as 'la critique d'une certaine poésie de mots plutôt que d'idées . . .' (O.C. I, 24):

Honneur sans doute au rythme et à la rime, caractères primitifs et essentiels de la poésie. Mais ce qu'il y a de plus important, de fondamental, ce qui produit l'impression la plus profonde, ce qui agit avec le plus d'efficacité sur notre moral dans une œuvre poétique, c'est ce qui reste du poète dans une traduction en prose; car cela seul est la valeur réelle de l'étoffe dans sa pureté, dans sa perfection.

Even at his most subjective, Nerval is concerned with communication. He saw his most private dreams as gateways to an understanding of the reality that lay beyond the rational world, and felt that it was his duty to convey his glimpses of that reality to other men: 'c'est alors que je suis descendu parmi les hommes pour leur annoncer l'heureuse nouvelle' (*Aurélia*; I, 410). Thus the formal elements of his art were the servants of the message he had to convey, and 'beauty' for Nerval lay in the meanings of words, not in their forms.

One would expect, given his passionate interest in the world around him, that Nerval would have no difficulty in finding 'subjects', and that like Balzac he would be embarrassed only by the need for choice; but this is not the case. Nerval has been criticised for lack of invention. In his own lifetime he was so criticised by his biographer Mirecourt, who seems to have been quoting general opinion when he wrote of Nerval's work: 'ces livres, il faut en concevoir, pèchent du côté de l'invention . . .'[19] The same material was often used in several different publications, either wholly or in part, sometimes after a lapse of years;

and he drew much of his material from books, sometimes des-
scribing illustrations, often quoting or adapting anything from a
few sentences to quite lengthy passages.[20] Some of the experiences
he describes as his own were actually those of his friends or of
people he met on his travels.[21] All this might indeed mean that
he lacked ideas; it might equally mean that he was preoccupied
with a small number of themes and images which seemed to him
of overwhelming importance. Moreover his own comment on
invention is pertinent (*Les Nuits d'Octobre*; I, 79-80):[22]

Qu'ils sont heureux, les Anglais, de pouvoir écrire et lire des chapitres
d'observation dénués de tout alliage d'invention romanesque! . . .
　En effet, le roman rendra-t-il jamais l'effet des combinaisons bizarres
de la vie? Vous inventez l'homme, ne sachant pas l'observer.

Observation, as we have noted, means for Nerval imaginative
recreation of other people's experiences; if sometimes he
recounted them as if they were his own, it was because his vivid
imagination led him to identify himself with what he re-created:
'on arrive pour ainsi dire à s'incarner dans le héros de son
imagination, si bien que sa vie devienne la vôtre' (*Les Filles du
Feu*; I, 150). Besides, Nerval himself is not always to be identified
with the narrator in his works, any more than Marcel in *A la
Recherche du Temps perdu* is always to be identified with Proust.
His exploration of the experiences of others was a way of learning
about himself,[23] just as, when he eventually overcame his inhibitions and ventured to speak of his own experiences, he tried to
'étudier les autres dans moi-même' (*Promenades et Souvenirs*; I, 141).
His mother's death and the consequent difficult relationship with
his father complicated his view of the normal experiences of home
and family, and of love and friendship; for most of his life he did
not feel free to speak directly of what most concerned him. This
is, in my view, the reason for his long silence as a poet, for in
poetry it is more difficult to take refuge from one's self. But his
natural preoccupations were never far from his mind. His wide
and varied reading—so varied that the student of Nerval learns
not to be surprised at anything—was always directed by his
unconscious search for parallels to his own internal patterns and
for symbols to represent the ideas which obsessed him. Hence his
interest in works which appear trivial or inferior as literature or

art, but which for him were full of meaning. The elements of his inner world sometimes evolved freely in imagination, sometimes were unexpectedly mirrored in the world around him. They appear throughout his work both in their overt, acknowledged form and, much more often, in hints and suggestions which are all the more revealing for being inadvertent.

With age and failing health, his activities were increasingly restricted in scope. He thus found himself cut off from external sources of material, just as he entered into the 'age of retrospection', when depressions are liable to become more severe.[24] Nerval himself says: 'Les souvenirs d'enfance se ravivent quand on a atteint la moitié de la vie.—C'est comme un manuscrit palimpseste dont on fait reparaître les lignes par des procédés chimiques' (*Angélique*; I, 191). As Nerval entered middle-age, he became increasingly concerned with the sources of his experiences: 'C'est qu'il y a un âge,—âge critique, comme on dit pour les femmes,—où les souvenirs renaissent si vivement, où certains dessins oubliés reparaissent sous la trame froissée de la vie!' (*Promenades et Souvenirs*; I, 130). His mind became folded in on itself in an almost uninterrupted melancholy brooding, the lighter intervals were intoxicated and brief, and he found himself forced to come to terms with the problems he had been evading all his life. Those elements which had till then only found their way to the surface with difficulty, and often much disguised, were now seen for what they were, and he discovered that 'Inventer, au fond, c'est se ressouvenir' (*Les Filles du Feu*; I, 150-1). Perhaps he had always been dimly aware that this was so; almost ten years earlier he had written to Jules Janin: 'j'en ai assez de courir après la poésie; je crois qu'elle est à votre porte et peut-être dans votre lit' (I, 943). This inner source, though rich in poetry, seemed inadequate in his hours of depression: 'Ce que j'écris en ce moment tourne trop dans un cercle restreint', he wrote to Georges Bell in 1853; 'Je me nourris de ma propre substance et ne me renouvelle pas' (I, 1091). He was afraid of emptying his head completely, of having nothing left to write about: his epitaph, he wrote wryly to Mme de Solms, came to him 'du fond d'un cerveau vide' ('Madame et Souveraine'; I, 44).

The subjects of Nerval's writings, then, appear in the beginning only in half-involuntary hints, and force their way to the surface ever more strongly, until they dominate his mental field to the exclusion of all else. This achievement of full self-expression depends not on the acquisition of a perfected technique, but on a gradual development towards self-awareness and understanding, and it is important to remember that it is constant, and independent of his fluctuations of mood. If one forgets this, one may be tempted to divide the work into 'gay' and 'sad' pieces, whereas in fact it forms a unity, and is always 'about' the same experiences and responses.

The alternating periods of elation and depression in Nerval's life not only affect his capacity for thought and work, but also produce ambivalent emotional attitudes, since what seems possible, reasonable or desirable on one day may well, the mood altered, appear next day in a totally different light. Thus each and every preoccupation appears superficially in a double aspect in Nerval's work, according to the dominating mood; and neither aspect can be considered truer than the other: the 'truth', here, is precisely the constant ambivalence of attitude. Both halves of the temperament have equal value—indeed it is misleading to speak of the two 'halves' of his temperament, since the personality is a whole, only sometimes in sunlight and sometimes in shadow. By insisting on a gay Nerval ('le fol délicieux') or a gloomy one ('Nerval le nyctalope'), one may doubtless achieve a unified or 'logical' picture; yet the richness and variety of his work spring largely from his duality, and the powerful reverberations one feels, in the poems particularly, from the tensions it creates.

This basic duality of attitude can be observed in Nerval's use of certain key images. M. Jean Richer[25] has tried to demonstrate that the great figures of Nerval's mythology are examples of Jungian archetypes. This tells us only what is already clear: that he is dealing in the stuff of human life; it does not tell us how, or with what intention. Similarly, the articles in which François Constans compares Nerval's images with patterns of recognised spiritual significance can help us to appreciate the wide range of Nerval's art; but such comparison cannot by itself explain in what way his art is peculiarly his own, or how it is that when Nerval says 'une étoile', it means a star unlike the stars of any other poet.

The two central figures in Nerval's mythology are the fire-god and the siren-goddess. They appear constantly throughout his major works, and may be said to correspond roughly to a 'father' image and a 'woman' image (for the 'mother' image includes all women, as Isis is 'l'épouse et la mère sacrée'). Their characteristic duality may be clearly seen in a story, *La Reine des Poissons*, which is rarely considered to be of any importance in Nerval's work, but which is revealing precisely because its apparent impersonality allows Nerval a free and unguarded approach. *La Reine des Poissons* appears in *Les Filles du Feu* (sufficient indication, one would think, that it ought not to be overlooked) in the essay *Chansons et Légendes du Valois*, which follows *Sylvie*. It is the story of a boy who lives with his uncle, a woodcutter named Tord-Chêne, and of a little girl whose parents send her every day to fish in the river. The boy has not the heart to cut down living trees, and tries to satisfy his uncle with dead wood and bracken; the girl cannot bear to watch the fish dying, and puts them back in the river. On one day of the week, 'le même sans doute où la fée Mélusine se changeait en poisson', they do not meet; but on the next day the boy tells the girl that he saw her among the fish in the river, in the shape of a shining goldfish, and she says that as she swam along she saw him on the riverbank in the shape of a golden-topped oak-tree. Tord-Chêne finds them talking and beats the boy; he threatens the girl, saying that he knows she is 'la reine des poissons', and one day he will catch her in his basket and she will die. And so he does, but the boy recognises the gold-fish and tries to defend her. When his uncle tries to pull the boy away by his hair, he finds that the child is rooted in the earth. He goes to fetch his axe. He and his fellow-woodmen hack their way through the opposing trees to find the boy; the queen of the fish appeals to the rivers to stop them, for if the forests are destroyed the lakes and streams will dry up. The rivers flood the forest and drown the woodman. The little woodcutter and the fisher-girl become a sylph and an ondine and are reunited.

Why did Nerval select this story to represent the legends of the Valois? In general terms, its personification of the spirits of the woods and rivers must have appealed to his feeling that 'Tout est sensible'. But more specifically, the image of the 'reine des poissons' belongs to the series of images of the Siren which runs through Nerval's works. She is Octavie, 'cette fille des eaux', she is Mélusine, wife of Lusignan ('El Desdichado'), she is the Lorely of the Rhine, 'cette ondine fatale comme toutes les *nixes* du Nord qu'a chantées Henri Heine' (*Lorely*; II, 733); Pandora has a siren on her harp (I, 348),[26] and in Holland the Frisian girls who lure unwary customers into the cafés of the Kermesse 'sont aussi de la famille des antiques sirènes . . .' (*Lorely*; II, 833). Nerval agreed with Heine, for whom, he says, 'toute femme est . . . quelque peu nixe ou wili . . .' (O.C. I, 78). In *Promenades et Souvenirs* (I, 142) he speaks of Célénie, an avatar of Sylvie and of all the girls he remembered from his childhood, 'une petite paysanne qui m'a aimé et qui m'appelait son petit mari':

Célénie m'apparaît souvent dans mes rêves comme une nymphe des eaux, tentatrice naïve . . . découvrant, dans son rire enfantin . . . les dents de perle de la nixe germanique. Et certes, l'ourlet de sa robe était très souvent mouillé, comme il convient à ses pareilles . . . Elle aimait les grottes perdues dans les bois . . .

Nerval mentions that he was almost drowned in the Thève 'pour n'avoir pas voulu paraître poltron devant la petite Célénie!' There is a trace of fear and of resentment at the thought of the child whose whim had led him into danger. (He refers to the incident again in *Sylvie*; I, 264). The Siren is beautiful but cold, fascinating but deadly, like 'les chimères qui charment et égarent'; his life-long preoccupation with her image is summed up in 'El Desdichado': 'J'ai rêvé dans la grotte où nage la sirène . . .'

The figure of Tord-Chêne is one of many images of the fire-god, who is of capital importance in Nerval's work. Kneph ('Horus'), Antéros, Cain, Adoniram (in *Histoire de Soliman et de la Reine du Matin, Voyage en Orient*), all belong to this series, of which the prototype is the god Vulcan, the artist and blacksmith, the lame husband of Venus: 'le boiteux'. All are images of one aspect or another of Nerval's feelings for his father, who was also lame. Sometimes the fire-god is Kneph, 'l'époux farouche'; sometimes he is Adoniram the artist, lord of the element of fire, 'fils du feu', and in this aspect he becomes also the poet himself, who tried increasingly, as he grew older, to identify himself with his father: 'plus j'avance en âge, plus je sens de toi en moi' (Letter to his father; I, 1127). In *La Reine des Poissons*, the figure of Tord-Chêne is related to another blacksmith god, the Norse god Thor: he rushes from his hut, axe in hand, 'menaçant, terrible et trans-figuré comme un fils d'Odin; dans sa main brillait cette hache scandinave qui menace les arbres, pareille au marteau de Thor brisant les rochers' (I, 283). He wields unjust authority over his nephew, whose power he has usurped, and forces him to follow a profession he hates. As in the case of the 'uncle' in *La Pandora*, is there not a reference here to Nerval's father, who was a strict authoritarian, who withheld from his son the marriage portion of his dead wife, which should have gone to the boy, and who insisted that Nerval become a doctor like himself? The suggestion seems to be reinforced by Nerval's explicit disclaimer, added to the story at its first publication in 1850: 'Nous ne pensons pas qu'il faille voir dans cette légende une allusion à quelqu'une de ces usurpations si fréquentes au moyen-âge . . .' (I, 1245). The thought had evidently crossed his mind.

Nerval's resentment never expressed itself openly, no doubt because, like all his emotions, it was not unmixed with feelings of quite another kind. There are many indications that Nerval respected, admired and in some ways envied his father, and that despite all the difficulties between them, he continued to love him. In the *Mémorables*, therefore, the blacksmith god is pardoned with the rest (*Aurélia*; I, 411):

Malheur à toi, dieu-forgeron, qui as voulu briser un monde!
  Cependant, le pardon du Christ a été aussi prononcé pour toi!
  Sois donc béni toi-même, ô Thor, le géant,—le plus puissant des fils d'Odin!

Pardon and reconciliation—the achievement of harmony—was the goal of all Nerval's activities; but for him such reconciliation was not, as it is for so many of us, merely a matter of comfortable compromise, of avoiding unpleasantness. Because of the changing aspect of the world as he saw it, he was faced with the necessity of making sense of apparent contradictions, and of learning to love all creation, as he said Heine loved woman, 'malgré ses défauts et surtout à cause de ses défauts'. That difficult objective underlies the best of his work, in poetry or in prose.

THE POETICAL WORKS

To most readers, Nerval's sonnets, *Les Chimères*, appear at first to be a poetic experience of so unusual a nature that there is a temptation to think of them as being singular and entirely self-sufficient. This view is not without justification, for despite the similarities of theme and image (and they are many) between these sonnets and the rest of Nerval's work, there remains a very strong sense that the rest of the work is of a different order. One can nevertheless trace a line of development throughout Nerval's career as a poet. His poems, if we discount the ones he wrote while still at school, are very few in number, and of these only a handful are generally considered worthy to stand beside *Les Chimères*; but if one takes them together with his translations and his writings on poetry and music, one can see the evolution of a conception of poetry which contributes to the character of *Les Chimères*, even if it cannot explain their unique intensity.

Nerval's poetical works were never collected during his lifetime. The nearest he came to making such a collection was in *Petits Châteaux de Bohême* in 1853, where his reminiscences of the period of the Doyenné are interspersed with groups of verses, all of which had been previously published in various journals or formed part of the libretti of *Piquillo* and *Les Monténégrins*. He omitted all his earliest work, and also a small number of poems published in journals between 1828 and 1832, mostly adaptations of poems by Thomas Moore, which he had based on French translations of the English text. In *Petits Châteaux de Bohême* the poems are divided into two groups, one following the 'Premier Château', and one the 'Troisième Château'. (The 'Second Château' is followed by the one-act prose play, *Corilla*, which was subsequently included in *Les Filles du Feu*.) The eleven poems in the first group, to which Nerval gives the title *Odelettes*, were all published individually between 1830 and 1835; the group entitled *Mysticisme*, which follows the 'Troisième Château', contains three poems which were first published in *L'Artiste* in 1844 and 1845, and which were incorporated into *Les Chimères* in 1854: 'Le Christ aux Oliviers', 'Daphné' (later retitled 'Delfica') and 'Vers Dorés'. These are followed by a small final group of short poems, entitled *Lyrisme*.

The interesting thing about this history is the fact that Nerval, whom we now consider primarily as a poet, did not apparently intend that his contemporaries should regard him as a poet at all. His early volumes of verse appeared before 1826, but after 1828, when he achieved fame as the translator of *Faust*, he published no more poems in book form, and very few in reviews. His finest work, *Les Chimères*, did not appear until a year before his death, and then it forms the appendix to a book of stories, *Les Filles du Feu*. It seems moreover to have been forced from him by circumstances which he was much inclined to regret.[1] Certainly, throughout his career, he devoted a great deal of thought to the nature of poetry: his reflections may be found in his introductions to the poetry of the sixteenth century (1828) and to his translations of German poets (1830); in the preface to his translation of *Faust* (1840); in the essays on Heine accompanying his versions of Heine's *Intermezzo* and *Nord-See* (1848); and in his studies of folksong. Poetry always seemed to him to be the highest form of literature, because it was the form most capable of expressing the real concerns of the human spirit. It may well have been partly because of his exalted conception of the rôle of poetry that he was diffident about publishing his own efforts; but there were other factors at work as well.

With the exception of the three poems to which he later gave the general title of *Mysticisme*, those verses which Nerval published at intervals in various journals are accomplished and charming (in one or two cases something more), but in general they show very little evidence of an original poetic genius. The text of *Petits Châteaux de Bohême* introduces them with a light-hearted account of the poet's youthful experiences, which does little to illuminate the poems. He refers to them as 'juvenilia', and wonders whether 'ces poésies déjà vieilles ont encore conservé quelque parfum'. The tone of these passages gives to the verses the air of slightly faded relics, charmingly sentimental, like pressed flowers in an old diary. The reader has the impression that he is not to take them too seriously. This part of the text first appeared in *L'Artiste* in 1852, under the title *La Bohême galante*.

In 1853, in *Petits Châteaux de Bohême*, Nerval added a new short paragraph to introduce a further group entitled *Mysticisme*. The markedly different nature of these three poems is explained, in this paragraph, by cryptic references to their source in an unhappy love affair, to *désespoir*, *fièvre* and *insomnie*: 'Une longue histoire, qui s'est dénouée dans un pays du nord,—et qui ressemble à tant d'autres!' The allusion seems to be to the poet's fabled love for Jenny Colon, an impression which would have been reinforced for Nerval's readers in 1853 by the 'Premier Château', which recounts the tale of the unwritten opera *La Reine de Saba*, and by the 'Second Château', added in 1853, which introduces the text of *Corilla* with references to the illusory world of the theatre. Though obviously necessary as makeweight in what would otherwise have been a very slim volume, this play adds to the general atmosphere of illusion, gentle melancholy and humorous fantasy. Yet the three poems of *Mysticisme* have no obvious connection with an unhappy love affair at all. They appear to be poems of a 'philosophical' nature, concerned with the agony and resurrection of Christ, the immanence of God in nature, and the possible return of the pagan gods and of a lost Golden Age. One's feeling that they are concerned with matters quite foreign to the rest of the volume is only increased by the fact that Nerval follows them with four extremely slight examples of *vers d'opéra*.

The sub-title of *Petits Châteaux de Bohême* is *Prose et Poésie*. It looks like a mere description of the contents of the volume, but in fact it is something more. This curiously disjointed work is largely *about* prose and poetry, about their differences and their relative importance in Nerval's work. Not only does Nerval speak deprecatingly of the poems reprinted here, he also insists that he no longer writes poetry at all: 'il n'y a plus en moi qu'un prosateur obstiné'. After the failure of his plan to write a *Reine de Saba*, he tells us, 'la poésie tomba dans la prose'. The word *tomba* makes clear the relative value, in Nerval's eyes, of prose and poetry.[2] There is no reason to doubt these assertions, despite the appearance, in the following year, of *Les Chimères*. It is likely that most of these sonnets, though not perhaps all, were composed much earlier in Nerval's career, probably by 1844, and when Nerval wrote the first part of this text for *La Bohème galante* (1852), he may well have felt that he was unlikely to write any more poetry. In May 1854, some months after the publication of *Les Filles de Feu*, he wrote to Georges Bell from Strasbourg: 'Un prodige! En touchant les bords du Rhin, j'ai retrouvé ma voix et mes *moyens*! Hier soir, j'ai écrit un sonnet dans le trajet de Bade à Strasbourg . . .' This poem (which has not been identified, if it survived at all) seems to have been a sufficiently unusual event to warrant some excitement.

Nevertheless, though the writing of poetry occupied less and less of Nerval's time as he grew older, there is no doubt that he considered it to be the most important of his activities, despite the diffidence he expresses in *Petits Châteaux de Bohême*. A letter to his father, written from Vienna in 1839, discusses the relative importance he attached to the different aspects of his literary work (I, 827):

Le travail littéraire se compose de deux choses: cette besogne des journaux qui fait vivre fort bien et qui donne une position fixe à tous ceux qui la suivent assidûment, mais qui ne conduit malheureusement ni plus haut ni plus loin. Puis le travail des livres, du théâtre, l'étude de la poétique, choses lentes, difficiles, qui ont besoin toujours de travaux préliminaires fort longs et de certaines époques de recueillement et de travail sans fruit; mais aussi, là est l'avenir, l'agrandissement, la vieillesse heureuse et honorée.

He had no illusions about poetry: it was not something to be tossed off in an idle moment of inspiration; it required *travail*, *étude*, *recueillement*. Circumstances rarely favoured him; but it was poetry that he really cared about. In *Les Filles du Feu* he offers his sonnets to the reader with all his accustomed diffidence, but he adds firmly: 'la dernière folie qui me restera probablement, ce sera de me croire poëte: c'est à la critique de m'en guérir' (I, 159).

Why then was he so reluctant to publish his poems? Gautier once remarked that Nerval's object in writing of himself was generally to 'dérouter le lecteur', and it is probable that some motive stronger than modesty or the fear of being misunderstood (though these influenced him too) led Nerval to conceal his serious poetic work. The most likely explanation is that his finest poetry touched too closely on concerns that he preferred to keep private. In fact, he rarely spoke of himself at all until the last

year of his life. He was at first much disturbed by the publication
of Mirecourt's biography of him in 1854, as he explained in a
letter to Georges Bell (I, 1116); after a few days' reflection he
wrote to his father (I, 1122):

on m'y traite en héros de roman et c'est plein d'exagérations bienveillantes sans doute et d'inexactitudes qui m'importent fort peu du reste,
puisqu'il s'agit d'un personnage conventionnel . . . On ne peut
empêcher les gens de parler, et c'est ainsi que s'écrit l'histoire, ce qui
prouve que j'ai bien fait de mettre à part ma vie poétique et ma vie
réelle.

His life-long silence about his private affairs was evidently
deliberate.[3] Despite his reticence one can detect certain themes
which preoccupy him constantly; but equally constant was his
effort to keep them under control. Without the writings published
in the last year of his life: *Les Filles du Feu, Les Chimères* and *Aurélia*,
we would regard his earlier work as slight though pleasing, and
it is probable that we would fail to observe the presence of something deeper and darker.

The recurrence of underlying themes is less easily detected in
the poetry than in the prose work, for the fixed form of a poem
wholly encloses it, so that we are not inclined to see it as running
on into other poems or other works in a continuous utterance;
the borders of prose are less sharply defined in general, for the
writer as well as for the reader, and we can move more easily
among different texts, relating them to each other. The poem's
isolation is particularly felt in the sonnet, which has a physical
presence so solid and immediate that its fourteen lines present an
air of absolute finality, as if nothing could be added or taken
away. It is tempting therefore to see each of the sonnets of *Les
Chimères* as an object only loosely connected with the others, and
the whole group as detached from the rest of Nerval's poems.
However, certain familiar elements may be observed from the
very beginning.

As a poet, Nerval matured late. As we have seen, he set himself
high standards. He was aware of his tendency to absorb the
rhythms and diction of other poets and to reproduce them, more
or less unconsciously, in his own work. Imitation is the school
in which most poets learn their trade, as painters do, and it is a

rare poet who does not begin by imitating his predecessors. Nerval worked rapidly through a variety of 'influences', and though he was a gifted pupil he did not, in his early years, achieve a distinctive voice of his own. Besides those poems which were published, many more were preserved in notebooks, which Aristide Marie has described: 'Belle écriture régulière, vers bien alignés et scrupuleusement cotés, strophes disposées avec symétrie . . .'[4] Gisèle Marie adds that a typical notebook was 'orné d'un fleuron au titre . . . rehaussé çà et là d'en-têtes et de culs-de-lampe dessinés à la plume,—comme Gérard se plaira à en orner certains de ses manuscrits . . .'[5] There is a charming earnestness about the verses as a whole; but one would scarcely predict that their author might become an important and original poet. Technically they show an easy mastery of traditional models: classical alexandrines, epistles in the eighteenth-century manner, songs like Béranger's. But the subjects are conventional, and the treatment hardly less so; there are echoes of Horace, of Martial and of Byron—in short there is scarcely a line one would unhesitatingly ascribe to Nerval. His technique was precocious, but his emotional development was extremely slow.

Nerval's early fame was due rather to his success as a translator. Now the quality most essential in a successful translation is that elusive gift which the Germans call 'Sprachgefühl'—a feeling for language. It is clear that the young Gérard possessed this in unusually abundant measure; Mirecourt records that at school Nerval 'obtint toujours les premières places en version et les dernières en thème', and 'la version', he points out, 'veut du génie, le thème ne demande que de la patience . . .'[6] In Nerval's own early works, however, *génie* is decidedly lacking. What one finds is this same Sprachgefühl, applied to his native language: an ear for the characteristic movement of French prose and for the rhythms of French verse. He has as yet no strongly personal idiom: all his enthusiasms pass one by one into his work. The *Odelettes* are the first of his poems which may be considered to be truly characteristic, and even of these, Nerval said frankly: 'Je ronsardisais' (*Petits Châteaux de Bohême*; I, 73). This is not a question of straightforward 'imitation', however, for he did not consciously adopt the formal patterns of the Pléiade, but absorbed them, as it were musically: 'étant admise l'étude assidue de ces vieux poëtes, croyez bien que j'ai nullement cherché à en faire le pastiche, mais que leurs formes de style m'impressionnaient malgré moi . . .' (ibid.).

The use of conventional models indicates that Nerval was not consciously concerned, at this stage, with formal innovation; indeed, he was never at any stage in his career primarily interested in form. His ideas on the subject are rarely expressed, perhaps because he saw little need for discussing form as an entity; and it is entirely characteristic that when quoting an inscription on a fountain, he remarks: 'Je ne m'arrête pas à la forme des vers; c'est la pensée d'un honnête homme que j'admire' (*Angélique*; I, 228). One has glimpses of his feelings in such passages as that in which the artist Adoniram criticises art which limits itself to passionless imitation of outward forms (*Voyage en Orient*; II, 513):

Décadence et chute! tu copies la nature avec froideur . . . Enfant, l'art n'est point là: il consiste à créer . . . Souviens-toi des vieux Egyptiens, des artistes hardis et naïfs de l'Assyrie. N'ont-ils pas arraché des flancs du granit ces sphinx, ces cynocéphales, ces divinités de basalte . . .? En revoyant d'âge en âge ces symboles redoutables, on répétera qu'il exista jadis des génies audacieux. Ces gens-là songeaient-ils à la forme? Ils s'en raillaient . . . Mais le Dieu multiple de la nature vous a ployés sous le joug: la matière vous limite, votre génie dégénéré se plonge dans les vulgarités de la forme; l'art est perdu.

Art, for Nerval, is a passionate endeavour to feel and to re-create, in symbolic form, the reality of the life around us. Nerval acknowledged this power in Heine, and because of 'son incroyable puissance de réalisation', he placed Heine above Germany's greatest: 'On peut reprocher à Klopstock une fatigante profondeur, à Wieland une légèreté outrée, à Schiller un idéalisme parfois absurde; enfin, Goethe, affectant de réunir la sensation, le sentiment et l'esprit, pèche souvent par une froideur glaciale'; but in Heine, he says, 'l'idée et la forme s'identifient complètement; personne n'a poussé aussi loin le relief et la couleur . . . il passe devant vos yeux des tableux si impossiblement réels, que vous éprouvez une sorte de vertige' (O.C. I, 75).

Form, then, is only the outward expression of the life which the artist recreates; in itself it has no virtue. Nerval was not particularly impressed by formal *tours de force*. In his article 'Sur les Chansons populaires' (I, 460–1), he explicitly condemns such empty virtuosity in the field of music; we may assume that his views apply to poetry also, and indeed to all art:

Qu'un faiseur italien vole un air populaire qui court les rues de Naples ou de Venise, et qu'il en fasse le motif principal d'un duo, d'un trio ou d'un chœur, qu'il le dessine dans l'orchestre, le complète et le fasse suivre d'un autre motif également pillé, sera-t-il pour cela inventeur? Pas plus que poëte. Il aura seulement le mérite de la composition, c'est-à-dire de l'arrangement selon les règles et selon son style ou son goût particuliers.

There is a world of difference between Heine's 'puissance de réalisation' and such 'arrangement'.

In his earliest poems, Nerval expresses a preference for the classical in literature: 'repoussant le style Romantique / J'ose encor, malgré vous, admirer le classique . . .'[7] This resolves itself, however, as his characteristic dislike of a 'poésie de mots plutôt que d'idées':

> Fuis surtout, fuis toujours le style Romantique;
> Ah! fuis, il en est tems ces vers éblouissans;
> Où tout est pour l'éclat où rien n'est pour le sens . . .[8]

He has however no greater liking for the excessively formal 'classical' art which follows Malherbe, as he states with some force in his study of the sixteenth-century poets (O.C. I, 313):

l'art, toujours l'art, froid, calculé, jamais de douce rêverie, jamais de véritable sentiment religieux, rien que la nature ait immédiatement inspiré: le correct, le beau exclusivement; une noblesse uniforme de pensées et d'expression; c'est Midas qui a le don de changer en or tout ce qu'il touche.

It may seem paradoxical that both classical and romantic styles appear to arouse his dislike in some measure. But he disapproved of cold doctrine in any form: so that he rejects all kinds of theoretically calculated formal effect, whether its aim is romantic extravagance or classical restraint. He is ready to praise any art that seems to him to be fresh, spontaneous and human in its concerns. He regrets that 'il est arrivé qu'en France la littérature n'est jamais descendue au niveau de la grande foule', and prizes the folk-songs of the Valois more highly than the conventional products of the academic poets—'leurs odes, leurs épîtres et leurs poésies fugitives, si incolores, si gourmées' (*Chansons et Légendes du Valois*; I, 276).

Nerval felt strongly the fertilising power of the ancient folk-poetry of France, just as Goethe had been inspired by the German Volkslied. In his study of the influence of folk-song on the Romantic poets, Tiersot says of Nerval: 'Il a noté . . . les poésies de ces chansons conservées sur la terre natale : cela était vraiment nouveau à l'époque où il est venu . . . Gérard de Nerval a donc joué, en cela, le rôle d'un initiateur'.[9] Nerval welcomed the idea of a collection of regional songs ('Sur les Chansons populaires'; I, 461): 'Là, sans doute, nous pourrons étudier les rythmes anciens conformes au génie primitif de la langue, et peut-être en sortira-t-il quelque moyen d'assouplir et de varier ces coupes belles mais monotones que nous devons à la réforme classique.'

It must not be imagined however that it was through its superficial simplicity of form that the folk-song commended itself to Nerval. The simplicity is often only apparent, and the sources of folk-poetry are frequently to be found in the work of difficult and non-popular poets (that is to say, those who do not intentionally appeal to the widest public): Nerval himself notes that Ronsard's *Odelettes* 'se chantaient et devenaient même populaires' (*Petits Châteaux de Bohême*; I, 73-4); and the lyrics of the Spanish poet Lorca were widely adopted as folk-songs in his lifetime, a process which he viewed with consternation. It was a compliment which Nerval would have known how to appreciate, for a people adopts in this way only what accords with its profoundest nature. What Goethe found in the Volkslieder, and Nerval in his Valois songs, was a measure of humanity, fresh and unspoiled, such as literature and society had both long disdained to offer, a transcendent simplicity of feeling. Some of the Valois folk-songs are quoted in *Angélique*, where, as in *Sylvie*, they are constantly linked with the idea of childhood innocence and happiness. Nerval quotes many more of the songs in various essays; scholars have neglected them, he suggests, because they are written in 'la vraie langue française', but with what seems to be a shocking carelessness in matters of syntax, prosody and rhyme. Not having the strangeness or quaintness of dialect, they seem merely ignorant.

He defends the folk-song stoutly in lines which tell us a great deal about his own preferences in poetry (*Chansons et Légendes du Valois*; I, 275): 'ces charmantes et naïves productions de poètes modestes . . . ces hardiesses ingénues . . . Quoi de plus pur d'ailleurs comme langue et comme pensée . . .' He regrets that French poetry is restricted by its academic outlook to the production of conventional 'bouquets à Chloris'. He regrets even more the fact that the people of the countryside are beginning to sing 'les romances à la mode', and laments 'une foule de petits chefs-d'œuvre qui se perdent de jour en jour avec la mémoire et la vie des bonnes gens du temps passé' (ibid.; I, 284). It is a kind of betrayal, like that of Sylvie when she refuses to sing a folk-song for the narrator, and begins 'un grand air d'opéra moderne . . . Elle *phrasait*!' (I, 265).

Genuine emotion was as vital to Nerval's conception of artistic value as it was to his own well-being. As he grew older and more aware of his emotional difficulties, his own poems turned from the expression of his adolescent enthusiasms to a concern with the nature of emotion itself. A change in manner is evident for the first time in those poems which Nerval grouped together under the title of *Odelettes* in *Petits Châteaux de Bohême*. Some of these poems are recognisably Nerval's, especially 'Une Allée du Luxembourg', 'Fantaisie' and 'Les Cydalises' (I, 16, 18, 26). All have the same theme: loss, nostalgia for the thing lost, and a dream-like awareness of its continued existence in some rarely accessible sphere. This theme appears in a passage of *Faust* and is discussed by Nerval in his Preface to the 1840 edition of his translation of Goethe's play; it is obvious from the tone of his comments on this passage that he has selected it because of its nearness to his own concerns. For Goethe, he says (O.C. I, 13–14),

comme pour Dieu sans doute, rien ne finit, ou du moins rien ne se transforme que la matière, et les siècles écoulés se conservent tout entiers à l'état d'intelligences et d'ombres, dans une suite de régions concentriques, étendues à l'entour du monde matériel. Là, ces fantômes accomplissent encore ou rêvent d'accomplir les actions qui furent éclairées jadis par le soleil de la vie, et dans lesquelles elles ont prouvé l'individualité de leur âme immortelle. Il serait consolant de penser, en effet, que rien ne meurt de ce qui a frappé l'intelligence, et que l'éternité conserve dans son sein une sorte d'histoire universelle, visible par les yeux de l'âme, synchronisme divin, qui nous ferait participer un jour à la science de Celui qui voit d'un seul coup d'œil tout l'avenir et tout le passé.

Though the *Odelettes* are characteristic of Nerval both in tone and in theme, he had not yet reached the best of which he was capable. Those few of the *Odelettes* which prefigure *Sylvie*, for instance, entirely lack the essential insight and self-awareness of *Sylvie*. The emotions fill the whole range of Nerval's vision, and they are consequently expressed as absolutes, simply, directly, and without comment or reservation. In 'Une Allée du Luxembourg' the poet writes 'Le bonheur passait,—il a fui!'; when he came to write *Sylvie* he was much less certain: 'Là était le bonheur peut-être; cependant . . .' (I, 273). At the time when he was writing the *Odelettes*, experience had not yet become a problem for Nerval, so that he does not examine or analyse his emotions, but simply records them. The question-marks and ambiguities which are so persistent a feature of *Les Chimères* are entirely absent from the early poems. But the *Odelettes* remain in the mind nonetheless. Their melancholy has an unaffected sweetness that is peculiarly attractive, and their relaxed harmoniousness makes a perfect foil for the tense counterpoint of *Les Chimères*.

In the middle years of his career Nerval seems to have been less able to write poetry. It is difficult to date the sonnets of *Les Chimères* with any precision, but by 1845 he had published 'Le Christ aux Oliviers', 'Delfica' and 'Vers Dorés', and it is likely that others of this group of sonnets had already been written by that date.[10] A great deal of Nerval's time, during this period, was devoted to the theatre, to his *feuilletons*, and to the writing of prose, including an unfinished novel (*Le Marquis de Fayolle*) and accounts of his travels to Vienna and the Middle East. The next manifestation of poetic activity which we can date is not a poem of his own but his translations of Heine's poems. Like his earlier translation of Goethe's *Faust*, this work is of profound importance in his own development as a poet, for it is not simply a transliteration, but an imaginative recreation of the original, in the course of which Nerval was exercising his own mastery over words and extending his conceptions of what poetry could say and do. When he came to write his last poems, it was with a much greater confidence in his own powers. There is an obvious change in manner between 'Le Christ aux Oliviers', for instance, and 'El Desdichado' or 'Artémis', a change which cannot be accounted for simply in terms of external influences. The difference is one of intention: the first of the sonnets to be published, like Nerval's early poems, seek to contain the poet's ideas and emotions within a conventional mould, thus rendering them acceptable to the reader of Nerval's time; the last of the sonnets are concerned with exploring and expressing an experience so intense and so personal that the mould must be altered to fit. The three poems which Nerval included in *Petits Châteaux de Bohême* under the title of *Mysticisme* might not, in this context, seem radically different from 'Fantaisie' or 'Les Cydalises'; but the other sonnets would have produced, among the discreetly elegant verses in that volume, the effect which Nerval expected from the intrusion of dramatic realism into the world of classical tragedy: 'Trop souvent un personnage, un détail *vrai*, risqueraient de tout bouleverser, tout confondre, ainsi qu'Enée en voulant monter vivant dans la barque des morts, lui fit faire eau de toutes parts et mit en fuite au bruit de son armure *vraie* les ombres errantes sur le bord du Styx'.[11] The presence of *Les Chimères* as a whole in *Petits Châteaux de Bohême*, quite apart from the difficulties of presenting them to the reader, would have revealed the other poems for what they are: talented, charming, and mostly rather slight. The sonnets stand on their own in Nerval's work, as he saw himself, and while one may detect the prefiguration of some of their themes in earlier poems, nothing in those earlier poems prepares one for the unique force of diction, image, rhythm and rhyme of *Les Chimères*, nor for the poet's searching examination of the limits at once of poetic utterance and of human understanding. It seems likely that Nerval withheld the sonnets from publication for two reasons: first, because he was aware that their use of language and of poetic image would strike his contemporaries as strange, and possibly unbalanced (and here one must remember that in 1841 Jules Janin had deeply offended Nerval by his premature obituary and that thereafter Nerval was always worried that his sanity might be questioned); and secondly, because these poems reveal so much, when one learns to read them, of the essential problems of the poet's life. Even in

1854, he tried to defend them against exegesis with the disarming remark: 'Ils ne sont guère plus obscurs que la métaphysique d'Hégel ou les *Memorables* de Swedenborg, et perdraient de leur charme à être expliqués, si la chose était possible . . .' Some readers, as we shall see, have gratefully heeded his warning, while others have understandably regarded it as a challenge. My own feeling is that in asking to be granted at least 'le mérite de l'expression', Nerval was pointing the way to a proper understanding of *Les Chimères*: neither as riddling rhymes nor as disembodied music, but as the outward expression of an inward thought, a form of words matched, as exactly as his poetic talent allowed, to an idea.

What that idea was, and what emotions it created in the poet, is not easily perceived on cursory reading, especially if the reader concentrates his attention on a single sonnet. Nerval wrote in his introduction to *Les Filles du Feu* that since Dumas had rashly printed one of the sonnets ('El Desdichado'), 'il faut que vous les entendiez tous' (I, 158). It was evidently essential that the unity of the group should be preserved, if the sonnets were to be properly appreciated.

Some of the themes which run through the group as a whole are those which we have already seen in 'Fantaisie' and 'Les Cydalises'. There are expressions of loss and grief: 'ces dieux que tu pleures' ('Delfica'), 'c'est la mort—ou la morte . . .' ('Artémis'), 'ma seule *etoile* est morte' ('El Desdichado'); and as in the earlier poems, the past is made present by the action of memory: 'Reconnais-tu le TEMPLE' ('Delfica'), 'Je pense à toi . . .' ('Myrtho'), 'Rends-moi le Pausilippe . . .' ('El Desdichado'). But added to these there is a much more sombre note. There are hints of violence and anger in 'Artémis', 'Horus', 'Myrtho' and 'Antéros'. There are doubts and unresolved questions in 'Le Christ aux Oliviers' and 'Delfica', which are more easily detected when these sonnets are placed beside the conflicts of 'Antéros' and 'Horus'. There is unmistakable anguish in 'Artémis', and profound melancholy in 'El Desdichado'. These darker emotions indicate a radical uncertainty in the poet, which leads him to pass his experience in review and to try to elicit its meaning. Thus in 'Artémis' he questions his own and his lover's identity, and the nature of love itself; he remembers, in 'Myrtho', an idyllic love which is followed by dust and ashes; he imagines, in 'Horus' and 'Antéros', a perfect consummation which seems precarious and threatened; in 'Delfica' he predicts the return of the golden age, though it is not yet come; in 'Artémis' he affirms his belief in an abiding love which he sees nonetheless as both *délice* and *tourment*. If these sonnets seem ambiguous, it is because duality is at their very heart; the alternation of bright and dark which governed the poet's life is reflected in *Les Chimères*. Yet the sonnets are not disordered, for as the poet's confusions are controlled by the sonnet's form they acquire both pattern and meaning. At the end of his introduction to *Les Filles du Feu*, Nerval remarks (I, 159): 'la dernière folie qui me restera probablement, ce sera de me croire poëte'. It was, as we have seen, a title which throughout his life he had hesitated to claim. Clearly, he felt that the sonnets of *Les Chimères* enabled him at last to describe himself as a poet; they are indeed, as he must have recognised, poetic in the highest sense. The poet 'A.E.' (George Russell) once remarked to the young James Joyce: 'I do not think you have chaos enough in you to make a world'. The chaos in Nerval was sufficient to have defeated most men; through his steadfast faith in the power of the 'lyre d'Orphée', he created from it a coherent world of order and of harmony.

THE TRANSLATIONS

Nerval's translation of *Faust* (Part I), which was published in 1828, already shows the qualities characteristic of his translations of poetry. His version of Goethe's drama is largely in prose, though he made verse translations of the ballad 'Der König in Thule' and of Gretchen's song at the spinning wheel ('Meine Ruh' ist hin'). The prose is however of a subtly poetic nature; restrained and rhythmical, it catches the nuances of Goethe's verse, conveying a sense of the beauty and force of the original which is rare in a translation. Berlioz used this version as the basis for the libretto of his *La Damnation de Faust* in 1846.

In 1830 Nerval published *Poésies allemandes*, a collection of translations from Bürger, Klopstock, Goethe, Schiller and others. The vogue in France, from about 1830 onwards, was for the 'fantastique' in German literature, in particular for the stories of E. T. A. Hoffmann.[1] Nerval shows only a passing interest in this aspect, though it is possible to see the influence of Hoffmann's style in some of his work, in *Les Nuits d'Octobre*, for instance, or at a greater distance in *La Pandora*. Typically, Nerval uses fantasy only in the cause of a more perfect realism, never for its own sake; in *La Pandora* for example, the fantastic elements are there to make the reader feel how precarious is the narrator's hold on his emotions. What interests Nerval is the how and the why of real experience, and in his study of the German poets in 1830 he is characteristically and unfashionably concerned with a poetry of ideas, about love, life and death, about man and nature, and about the rôle of poetry itself in a rapidly changing world.

Nerval's introduction to the translations quotes at length from Mme de Staël's *De l'Allemagne*, and most of the poems he translates are summarised or referred to in Mme de Staël's text (Part II, Chapter XIII). But the summaries in *De l'Allemagne*, while they show the German poets' interest in ideas, convey almost nothing of the effective force of the originals. The images of the German poets especially are weakened when deprived of the interaction of meaning and rhythm, and of the effect of the word-sounds in the original German. Nerval's translations draw on both his feeling for language and his understanding of emotional complexities, and his versions of the German lyric poets show the same felicitous turn of phrase as the translation of *Faust*; they manage to make one feel (as one should) the essential 'foreignness' of the German poems while at the same time they express the ideas and images of the German writers in terms acceptable to the French reader. If these translations have been acclaimed as superior to any produced in France before this date,[2] it is probably because Nerval understood, and was careful to preserve, the differences between French and German poetry. He insists, in his introduction to the translations (O.C. I, 35) that he has been chiefly concerned with fidelity to the originals—it is the same principle which governed his transcriptions of French folk-songs: 'j'offre ici des traductions de vif enthousiasme et de premier jet, que je n'ai peut-être pas réussi à faire bonnes, mais qui du moins sont exactes et consciencieuses. Les jugements tout faits n'avancent rien en littérature; des traductions fidèles peuvent, je crois, davantage. Quant aux imitations, on n'en veut plus, et on a raison'. In the introduction, Nerval makes an important distinction between French and German poetry which recalls his comparison between Goethe the theorist and Heine the poet of imagination:[3] 'chez nous c'est l'homme qui gouverne son imagination . . . chez les Allemands c'est l'imagination qui gouverne l'homme, contre sa volonté, contre ses habitudes, et presque à son insu' (O.C. I, 35). These observations, and the comments on individual poets, show that even at this stage Nerval was quite sure of what he was looking for in art. He rejects the rigidity of French classical doctrine, and praises in German poetry 'un univers magique . . . un vrai chaos, soit! du ridicule souvent à force de sublime . . ., ou bien un monde, tout un monde spirituel, aussi vrai qu'il est possible de l'inventer'; through this new creation the poet was to disturb the reader's 'confort intellectuel':

lisez-le superficiellement, avec vos préventions de collège, et sans songer que vous n'êtes plus en France, sans rappeler à vous vos illusions de jeune homme, et les singulières pensées qui vous ont assailli parfois dans une campagne au clair de lune, et bientôt vous aurez jeté le livre avec le mépris d'une curiosité trompée, et vous serez rentré dans votre cercle de pensées habituelles, en murmurant comme un homme qu'on a troublé dans son sommeil.

In this estimate of the purpose of poetry, as in his judgements of individual poets, Nerval shows his independence of current fashions, and a firm adherence to his own values, which are as always moral rather than primarily aesthetic. An example of his personal preferences can be seen in his comparison of Goethe with Schiller. In Nerval's time Goethe was generally held to be the greatest of all German poets;[4] Schiller occupied a strictly secondary place as a lyric poet, although his dramas were admired. Nerval reverses this judgement, and for characteristic reasons: 'Goethe . . . pèche souvent par une froideur glaciale . . .', he wrote in an essay on Heine (O.C. I, 75); 'le maître veut rester indifférent à tout, et ne veut que peindre . . . dès qu'il se met à faire des vers, il revêt son habit d'architecte, de peintre et de statuaire, et fait son travail à son aise, sans se donner beaucoup de peine et sans s'abandonner comme Schiller, qui, à chaque ligne, à ce qu'il prétend, perdait une goutte de sang' (*Les Poètes allemands*, 1840; O.C. I, 64). It is the same rejection of the primacy of form which we have seen in his essays on folk-poetry and music, and the same assertion of the value of feeling. Much as he admired the grandiose conceptions of destiny and love which he found in *Faust*, Nerval's first interest was in humanity and human passions of a more intimate, suffering kind; because of this preference, he was inclined to place Heine first among German poets.

Nerval translated Heine's poems over a long period ending with the publication in the *Revue des Deux Mondes* (15 July and 15 September 1848) of *La Mer du Nord* (*Nordsee*) and *Intermezzo*. He chooses to analyse, in his introductions to these works (O.C. I, 72–90), only those poems whose subject is close to his own preoccupations. All of them are concerned with illusion, with love and the pain of loving, with dream as an extension of experience, with memory, and with poetry as the expression of passion and as the source of understanding—for how can we understand what we cannot express? Barker Fairley, remarking on the repeated use of 'the song within the song' in Heine's work, suggests that no other poet so constantly wrote poems about the

writing of poetry.[5] Nerval, who resembles Heine in so many
ways, resembles him in this also. The theme of song and of poetry
runs through all his work, from 'Fantaisie' ('Il est un air pour qui
je donnerais Tout Rossini, tout Mozart et tout Weber . . .') to the
'chanson d'amour' of 'Delfica' and the music of the 'lyre
d'Orphée' in 'El Desdichado'. Like Heine, Nerval was very
consciously a poet; and it is because of this similarity of attitude,
as well as their temperamental likeness, that he felt so much in
sympathy with Heine's work. His translations catch the spirit of
the originals to a quite remarkable degree. They even succeed
in catching something of Heine's music, although again Nerval
makes no attempt to reproduce the metrical forms of the original
texts: both the *vers libre* of *Nordsee* and the regular stanzas of
Intermezzo are transcribed into a measured prose. The originality
of this 'prose poétique' may not be appreciated by the modern
reader, whose ear has grown accustomed to such cadences; but
we have only to compare the rhythmic subtlety of Nerval's
version with the flexibility of Heine's use of metre, to see with
what art Nerval has analysed and reproduced Heine's effects. It
is not, of course, only for their technical brilliance that these
translations are so admirable. Heine himself said of Nerval:
'Cette âme était essentiellement sympathique, et sans comprendre
beaucoup la langue allemande, Gérard devinait mieux le sens
d'une poésie écrite en allemand que ceux qui avaient fait de cet
idiome l'étude de toute leur vie . . .'[6] What makes these translations something more than a technical *tour de force* is the compassionate humanity which the reader feels in them. They must
be counted among the finest of Nerval's works, for he brought
to them, as to his own poetry, not only an exceptionally sensitive
'Sprachgefühl', but also a sensitive heart.

V

LES FILLES DU FEU

When the volume containing *Les Filles du Feu* and *Les Chimères* was published in January 1854, Nerval was in Dr Emile Blanche's asylum, where he had been a patient since August 1853. Throughout 1852 he had been anxiously trying to collect his scattered writings into a number of volumes, to be published as his 'complete works'. In a short interval between two periods of mental disturbance in 1853 he had managed to complete a new work, *Sylvie*, and to prepare it for publication in the *Revue des Deux Mondes*. He decided, late in 1853, to collect in one volume certain other prose works which he had published previously. Jean Richer (I, 743) and Léon Cellier (in his edition of this text) both suggest that the core of the volume is formed by the play *Corilla*, the article *Isis*, and the story *Octavie*; these three pieces have a Neapolitan background which recurs in *Les Chimères* in references to *le Pausilippe, la mer d'Italie, le laurier de Virgile*, and *le volcan*. To these Nerval added his adaptation (dating from 1843) of a German original, *Jemmy*; from 'Les Faux-Saulniers' (first published in *Le National* in 1850, and already robbed of some of its chapters to make 'l'Histoire de l'abbé Bucquoy' in *Les Illuminés*), he took a section to which he gave the name of *Angélique*; and he included another very early work, a story written by Auguste Maquet to Nerval's scenario, which had been published in *Le Messager* (1839) with the title 'Le Fort de Bitche': the title was now altered to *Emilie* to match the Christian-name titles of the other pieces in the collection. At a very late stage in the production of the volume, Nerval decided not to include *La Pandora*, which was unfinished, and after some hesitation *Sylvie*, by far the best of the pieces in *Les Filles du Feu*, was added to make up the weight; with it came *Chansons et Légendes du Valois* (a new name for a study of folk-poetry already published six times in various versions), and *La Reine des Poissons* (a Valois legend which Nerval had already used on three occasions). In this volume there also appeared for the first time the whole group of *Les Chimères*; three of these eight poems had been published many years before (and were reprinted in *Petits Châteaux de Bohême* in January 1853); one, 'El Desdichado', had appeared quite recently.

The introduction to *Les Filles du Feu* (*A Alexandre Dumas*; I, 149–59) is in the form of a letter; it contains a long fragment recounting the history of one Brisacier whose illusory love echoes both *Octavie* and *Sylvie*, and who describes himself in terms which recall 'El Desdichado': 'Moi . . . le prince ignoré, l'amant mystérieux, le déshérité, le banni de liesse, le beau ténébreux . . .'; moreover Brisacier likens himself and his beloved to Le Destin and L'Etoile, characters in Scarron's *Roman comique*: 'Le Destin' is the alternative title on the Eluard manuscript of 'El Desdichado', in which the poet laments the death of 'ma seule *étoile*'.

Brisacier's story, like most of the material in the volume, had been published earlier. It appeared in *L'Artiste* under the title of 'Le Roman tragique' in 1844, two years after the earliest version of the central episode of *Octavie* had been published in *La Sylphide* ('Un Roman à faire'; 1842). The theme of the 'seigneur poète' accredited to a company of actors and hopelessly in love with its 'froide étoile' makes its appearance again in *Sylvie* in 1853, and it seems likely that in *Sylvie* Nerval achieved a final working-out in prose of themes which had haunted him at least since 1842, and probably even earlier. These themes are also those of *Les Chimères*, and the sonnets are not arbitrarily linked with the prose pieces in *Les Filles du Feu*: they deal with the same ideas and the same experiences, but in a different way. The prose pieces themselves are not, as is often suggested, a miscellaneous collection.[1] Nerval has stressed the unity of the volume by giving to each separate piece the name of a woman or a goddess; these are the daughters of fire. It is not however immediately obvious what they have in common, and unless one considers the volume as a whole, it is difficult to see what characteristics of the element of fire these daughters of fire have inherited.

The Neapolitan landscape which forms the setting of some of the pieces in the collection is truly a 'terre du feu', volcanic and sunlit. The warmth and light of the Mediterranean have made it seem a place of spiritual rebirth and poetic inspiration to a long line of poets and artists from the beginnings of the Romantic movement until our own times; it appears in this rôle in *Les Chimères*. But there are darker elements in the poet's vision of this landscape. The volcano is as dangerous as the 'dieu des volcans' himself, who appears in 'Horus'; and the 'laurier de Virgile' in 'Myrtho' reminds us not only of classical harmony and the power of poetry, but of the fact that traditionally, the landscape around Naples is the landscape of Vergil's Hell in Book Six of the *Æneid*.[2] The word *chimère* has similar undertones: the Chimaera of classical legend was a fire-breathing monster which gave its name to a volcano on the seaboard of Ancient Greece; it appears in Roman poetry as one of the monsters of Hell. The duality of the 'terre du feu', source of life and place of damnation and death, is inherent in the nature of fire itself; for fire, since the earliest days of man, has been seen as a symbol of sexual potency and of the earth's fertility, yet it is dangerous if not controlled, and was always worshipped fearfully. We may surmise, then, that the character of the daughters of fire will be equally ambiguous. This is certainly true of the most illustrious of their race, who is not to be found in *Les Filles du Feu* at all; she is Balkis, the Queen of Sheba, who appears in *Histoire de Soliman et de la Reine du Matin* in *Voyage en Orient*. As Nerval portrays her, Balkis contains within herself all the contradictions implicit in the notion of a contact with fire. She is the light of morning, the kindler of passion and the promise of life; but she is also dangerous, and ultimately her lover Adoniram must die for the privilege of 'le baiser de la reine'.[3] This ambiguity is characteristic of the image of woman, and of the conception of love, in Nerval's writings.

A notable exception to the general view that *Les Filles du Feu* is a heterogeneous collection of pieces, only partly related to each other in imagery or background, is the suggestion of Jean Gaulmier[4] that the central theme of the collection is revolt: the more active heroines—Angélique, Jemmy, Corilla, Emilie—are in revolt against convention and determined to create their own destiny; the others—Aurélie, Octavie, Adrienne, Sylvie—are products of Nerval's own revolt, *chimères* with which he hoped to defy God and control his destiny. The attractive symmetry of this design should not blind us to the fact that it conceals a more simple and less fundamental division: the first four heroines are from stories in which Nerval is not directly involved as narrator-participant, the others from stories which are written in the first person and appear to be relating his own experiences. The theme of Promethean revolt is certainly present in *Les Chimères*. Prometheus himself, the fire-stealer, is mentioned in only one work: *La Pandora*, which Nerval originally intended to include in *Les Filles du Feu* and withdrew at the last moment. But rebellion is by no means the end of the story, even in *Les Chimères*; and in *Les Filles du Feu*, the poet is concerned, I think, less with the notion of revolt than with the search for some commanding ideal which can replace the discredited teachings of established religion. As he tells us in *Sylvie*, the most obvious and the most easily available surrogate was love.

At one stage, while he was preparing the manuscript of *Les Filles du Feu* for the printer, Nerval considered changing his proposed title to *Les Amours perdues* or *Les Amours passées* (Letter to Giraud; I, 1099). Of these, the second is purely nostalgic, but the first, which Nerval preferred, has a stronger and slightly different resonance. Nerval says that it would express 'le sentiment doux du livre', and adds 'et c'est plus littéraire, rappelant un peu *Peines d'amour perdues* de Shakespeare'. There is a difference between past love and lost love, especially if, as in *Love's Labour's Lost*, there is a suggestion of futility, of wasted emotion and the hopeless pursuit of illusion. That, I would suggest, is the theme which underlay Nerval's conception of *Les Filles du Feu*; it makes even stronger the links with *Les Chimères*, whose very name means 'illusions'. In the introduction to *Les Filles du Feu*, Nerval quotes from the remarks which Dumas had printed in *Le Mousquetaire* (10 December 1853) to introduce 'El Desdichado'. The sonnet had been printed without Nerval's permission at a time when the poet was in Dr Blanche's clinic, and Dumas had insinuated in his introduction that 'El Desdichado' was evidence of Nerval's insanity. In the passage cited by Nerval (I, 150), Dumas says that if Nerval is mad, then 'chacun désire le devenir pour suivre ce guide entraînant dans le pays des chimères et des hallucinations'. (Much energy has been expended on discussing the source of Nerval's title for his sonnets. It was a favourite word with him, but may he not also have been ironically taking his cue from Dumas?) Nerval goes on to explain the rôle of the imagination in his work. He is, he says, incapable of remaining detached from what he creates: 'on arrive pour ainsi dire à s'incarner dans le héros de son imagination, si bien que sa vie devienne la vôtre et qu'on brûle des flammes factices de ses ambitions et de ses amours!' For Dumas, he suggests blandly, the creation of fictional characters is 'un jeu'; for himself however it is 'une obsession, un vertige'. Believing that 'inventer, au fond, c'est se ressouvenir', he is led to conclude that what he 'invents' must be a vague memory of a past experience, perhaps in a former life (and here we recognise the theme of 'Fantaisie'): 'Le dix-huitième siècle même, où je m'imaginais avoir vécu, était plein de ces illusions' (I, 151). We need not take the suggestion of metempsychosis quite literally. But it is true to say that what Nerval 'invented' was always created out of his memories of past experience, including (and this is important) his literary experience. In time, then, because he knew how much illusion goes to the making of literature, he could see how much of what he had 'really' felt and believed had been illusion too. The theme of subjective illusion, and of passion expending itself in the vain pursuit of what never existed, is seen to run very strongly through *Les Filles du Feu*. More often than not, the fire is composed only of 'flammes factices'.

ANGÉLIQUE

First, and longest, of the pieces in the volume is *Angélique*. The construction of this story is complex and ingenious, and extremely characteristic of Nerval's narrative method. The text is presented in the form of twelve letters from Nerval to the editor of *Le National*[5]. The first letter recounts his adventures in search of a biography of the abbé de Bucquoy; he had seen the book in Frankfurt and had not bought it, thinking that he would find it in one of the libraries in Paris. Returning to Paris, he finds his fellow-writers trembling at a new regulation governing the press, which forbids the publication of what the law describes as a *feuilleton-roman*. Deciding to play safe and stick to historical fact, he announces the forthcoming publication of a biographical study of the abbé de Bucquoy: but the book cannot be found. Nerval sets out to track it down. There follows a diverting series of digressions within digressions, with mocking asides about censorship and officialdom, about librarians, scholars, literary gentlemen and all those who use and misuse libraries. Research in the police records at the Bibliothèque nationale leads, in the second letter, to his transcribing from them the dramatic moral tale of one Le Pileur (with the ironic introduction: 'Ce n'est pas un roman'). In the third letter, he tries the Bibliothèque Mazarine; the director believes the book is in the cellars among uncatalogued stocks. A short conversation with this gentleman gives Nerval the opportunity to mock the theatre censorship and to state emphatically that he is not interested in the 'roman historique, genre Dumas': 'Je n'en ai jamais fait; je n'en veux pas faire . . .' While waiting for news from the cellars, he decides to visit an old acquaintance at the Bibliothèque de l'Arsenal (which is, of course, officially closed for the holidays). On the way he is reminded of a ghost story (not fiction!) about a former curator of the Arsenal, which he proceeds to tell us; then, fearing that the ghost might be in residence during the vacation, he decides instead to try the antiquarian booksellers. He finds a biography of another, earlier Bucquoy, a soldier who may be the ancestor of the fantastic abbé; for, says Nerval (whose father was a soldier), 'les rêveurs succèdent aux hommes d'action'. Having spent all his money on this military epic, he is mortified, passing a *oiseleur* (again, the incident, however story-like, is presented as a real event, not fiction), to hear the merchant refuse to buy a bird in a cage from a distressed gentlewoman; Nerval wishes he had saved his money, so that he could help her. Finally he learns that a copy of the book he wants is to be auctioned at the end of the following month.

The fourth letter sees him impatiently consulting the Archives de France, where he finds an unpublished manuscript among the Bucquoy family papers, 'une trouvaille des plus heureuses': it contains the story of Angélique de Longueval, the great-aunt of the elusive abbé. The abbé's trail leads him to Compiègne—and we are suddenly in a dream world, where 'il est permis de rêver les plus belles bergeries du monde'. The library, of course, is closed—it is All Saints, and a public holiday; so he calls on one of the librarians, who shows him some rare manuscripts in his possession, one of which contains Rousseau's musical settings of songs. Nerval's delight in this rarity leads him to think of going back to Paris by way of Ermenonville, where Rousseau died. On the way (and Ermenonville can only be reached on foot for most of the way), he reflects on Angélique's story, which he now recounts at length. But the telling does not proceed uninterrupted. He has scarcely begun the fifth letter when he digresses at a critical point in the action (while disclaiming any intention of using the novelist's tricks to keep the reader in suspense!), in order to recount an adventure in Senlis, where he and a friend were almost arrested because they carried no papers. There follows a lyrical description of the countryside of his childhood and an invocation to the power of memory:[6]

je me repose en revoyant ces campagnes si vertes et si fécondes;—je reprends des forces sur cette terre maternelle.

Quoi qu'on puisse dire philosophiquement, nous tenons au sol par bien des liens . . . le plus pauvre garde quelque part un souvenir sacré qui lui rappelle ceux qui l'ont aimé. Religion ou philosophie, tout indique à l'homme ce culte éternel des souvenirs.

Nerval is obviously preoccupied now not only with Angélique's history, but also—perhaps chiefly—with his own. The sixth letter is entirely concerned with memories of his childhood; he remembers the village of Senlis, the songs the children sang, and a girl called Delphine who appeared as an angel in a school mystery play (an incident which recurs in *Sylvie*, where the girl is Adrienne). Abruptly, without transition of any kind, he returns briefly at the end of this letter to the story of Angélique. But at the beginning of the seventh letter he apologises for digressing yet again: he wants to give the reader some idea of the background to his story. One suspects that he is really being genuinely distracted from his tale by memories which he feels compelled to record—though of course he is also stretching his copy to fill another column or two. By way of background material, he transcribes a number of local folk-songs about fierce fathers and love-lorn daughters; they reflect the central theme of Angélique's captivity in her father's house: they also perhaps remind Nerval of his own authoritarian father.

The rest of the long seventh letter continues Angélique's story. The eighth letter begins with a digression on the history of the Valois, and its spirit of resistance against tyranny; it continues with Angélique's account of how she defied the world for the sake of love. The ninth letter adds details from other sources to complete the unfinished account in Angélique's own hand. The last three letters, interrupted by various anecdotes, are chiefly concerned again with Nerval's wanderings in the Valois and with his childhood memories; a rapid note at the end of the story tells us that he finally bought at auction the biography of the abbé de Bucquoy, and presented the volume to the Bibliothèque impériale (that is, the Bibliothèque nationale, where Nerval's gift now forms part of the reserve collection).

The last pages of *Angélique* place the story in the context of a long line of humorous moralists:

—Vous avez imité Diderot lui-même.
—Qui avait imité Sterne . . .
—Lequel avait imité Swift.
—Qui avait imité Rabelais.
—Lequel avait imité Merlin Coccaïe . . .
—Qui avait imité Pétrone . . .
—Lequel avait imité Lucien. Et Lucien en avait imité bien
    d'autres . . .

The structure of *Angélique* constantly diverts the reader's attention from Angélique herself and from her melancholy story, and does indeed give the narrative the air of a partly humorous, partly reflective tale, like Sterne's *Sentimental Journey*. But each time that Angélique's story emerges for a shorter or, rarely, a longer moment, it introduces a note of sadness and regret. Virtually a prisoner in her jealous father's house, she is naturally 'd'un caractère triste et rêveur'. Those who fall in love with her end badly, punished by her father or murdered by equally unlucky rivals. She runs away with a young man in her father's service, whose boldness pleases her; despite his low station, she feels he has 'le cœur très haut'; but, Nerval suggests, his splendid livery is partly to blame for 'l'illusion d'Angélique'. When the young man becomes a soldier, she follows his regiment, enduring many hardships and humiliations. Her lover proves to be both cruel and dissolute; after his death she eventually returns alone and destitute to her native village. But this is not, as Nerval constantly reminds us, 'un roman'; and consequently the emotions and reactions of the heroine are not simple. In the *Lettre à Alexandre Dumas*, Nerval suggests indirectly that one of his reasons for rejecting the novel (or at least, the 'roman historique, genre Dumas' of which he speaks in *Angélique*) is the falsity and super-ficiality of its treatment of emotion: 'on ne se perce pas le cœur avec une épée de comédie, on n'imite pas le cuisinier Vatel, on n'essaie pas de parodier les héros de roman, quand on est un héros de tragédie . . .' (I, 152). Angélique's tragedy is real, and the hallmark of its reality is the complexity of her emotional reactions. Thus while she may be the incarnation of the spirit of revolt, 'l'opposition même', she does not hate her father: 'Cependant elle aime son père,—et ne l'avait abandonné qu'à regret'.[7] Having once made her decision, however, she stands by it no matter what hardships it entails: 'du moment qu'elle avait choisi l'homme qui semblait lui convenir . . . elle n'a pas reculé devant la fuite et le malheur . . .'

Is it not likely that what attracted Nerval to Angélique's history was the parallel with certain aspects of his own life? His own mother followed her husband to the wars and suffered dreadful hardships: but in the case of Nerval's parents, it was the woman who died, the man who survived, and the child who was left to judge their decisions. In *Le Marquis de Fayolle* (1849) he had already considered the actions of a mother who abandons her child; he seems unable to understand how any woman could do such a thing: 'Comment a-t-elle pu vivre sans moi?' (I, 659). In *Angélique* he seems to be trying to enter imaginatively into the mind of a woman who is prepared, for the sake of the man she loves, to abandon all her previous affections. Furthermore, in the comment on Angélique's feelings for her father, her regret at leaving him even though she has chosen to follow her own path, there is an echo of many of Nerval's letters to his own father. Like Angélique, he was aware of 'une destinée qui ne peut être vaincue . . .' (I, 827), and made his choice firmly; yet when he left his father he wrote 'Que j'ai eu le cœur serré en te quittant . . .' (I, 1122).

What is certain is that Angélique was cruelly deceived. The great love for which she abandons all that she has known since childhood proves to be an illusion, and the source of endless sufferings and misery. Yet she does not reject it, not even when she has realised that she will never be happy, because she needs to believe that great love is possible. In her worst moment she writes gently: 'je sentais toujours mon affection aussi grande que lorsque nous partîmes de France. Il est vrai qu'après avoir reçu la première lettre de ma mère, cette affection se partagea en deux . . . Mais, j'avoue que l'amour que j'avais pour cet homme surpassait l'affection que je portais à mes parents'. Like the man in *Octavie*, the narrator in *Sylvie*, the young poet of *Elégies nationales*,[8] Angélique recognises the illusion for what it is, and continues to prefer it. It cannot make her happy. Worse, her devotion to the incarnation of her ideal is not even meaningful, for the real object of her affections never existed. But her loyalty, however futile, gives her a certain sad nobility.

SYLVIE

The construction of *Sylvie* (first published in 1853) is more truly complex than that of *Angélique*, though in a less obvious way. In *Angélique* the complexity is only apparent; though its movement is interrupted, and its mood broken by a large number of digressions, the story advances in a straightforward progression of events. The digressions remind us that the author is still there (it is a kind of 'alienation' affect), diverting our attention from his heroine to his own adventures, recent or past, his odds and ends of memory, hearsay, conjecture and fantasy; in this setting the story of Angélique herself appears less dark. In *Sylvie* the narration is not linear. The themes and images twist in and out, interlocking and diverging, turning back on themselves and reappearing, at each re-emergence subtly altered by the intervening movement, like the patterns of an orchestral fugue which are the same in shape yet different in tonality as they are taken up by different instruments. Apparently simple, the text begins on analysis to seem as intricate with possibility as a dream. We are transported from one period of time to another, from one place to another, sometimes by means of a journey, sometimes insensibly by the action of memory; sometimes both processes take place at once, as when the narrator, travelling to the Valois in a coach, lets his mind wander back in time to reach the Valois many years before the coach arrives. The characters in the story have the same dreamlike evanescence, appearing now in one guise, now in another: the narrator is a man, then a child, a youth, a younger man; Adrienne is in turn a vision, a memory, a ghost; Aurélie is 'une apparition' behind the footlights of a theatre, a mocking presence, a thoughtful woman who wants but fears to love—or perhaps she is only an echo of Adrienne; Sylvie is a child, a joyful girl, a poised and remote young woman, a contented wife and mother. These phantoms cross and re-cross each other's paths through a series of inconclusive confrontations from which none emerges as more durably real than the others; and the narrator himself cannot entirely grasp their reality.

The story is written in the first person, and many of its details seem to refer to Nerval's own life. But *Sylvie* is not a factual autobiography. Of less importance are the deviations, common enough even in avowedly biographical writing, from the known facts of Nerval's life; what matters is the poet's intention in writing his story. His adaptations and additions are not extraneous, they are the essence of the work; and they derive chiefly from his instinctive tendency to create a pattern where none, perhaps, was clearly visible before. This tendency might have operated at a purely literary level: that is to say, Nerval might have been solely concerned with the structure of his story, and with ordering events so that they produced a pattern within the literary form. In fact he tried sometimes to satisfy this instinct at a stage not only before the writing but even before the event, when he still had some choice: 'J'aime à conduire ma vie comme un roman', he wrote.[9] The word *conduire* reflects his constant desire to discern a structure in his life, and failing that to create one, to understand and hence to participate actively in his own destiny. He expresses the same desire in 'Paradoxe et Vérité' (1844; I, 429): 'diriger mon rêve éternel au lieu de le subir'. In *Sylvie* he is concerned not only with moulding his experience into a pleasing literary form, but with making sense of it.

The story begins in a theatre, where the narrator sits night after night, enslaved by an actress—or more precisely by the image of a woman. The first pages place us firmly in the world of illusion: the narrator appears 'en grande tenue de soupirant', like an actor dressed for his rôle; his beloved, radiant behind the footlights, sweet-voiced and beautiful, 'vivait pour moi seul'—but only for as long as they remained separated by the darkness between audience and stage. 'Depuis un an, je n'avais pas encore songé à m'informer de ce qu'elle pouvait être d'ailleurs; je craignais de troubler le miroir magique qui me renvoyait son image . . .' He is fairly certain that the reality would be less satisfying, having been warned by an uncle, who had recounted to him 'tant d'histoires de ses illusions, de ses déceptions', that actresses were not women, for 'la nature avait oublié de leur faire un cœur'. He prefers to devote himself to the image. The conscious illusion is safe, because we know it to be false; 'reality' is dangerous, because it proves to be only another illusion, and one against which we are defenceless, since we did not expect to be deceived.

At this point Nerval digresses from his own experience to offer us an anatomy of his times, in a remarkable paragraph that sums up in a few sentences the whole background to the Romantic movement in nineteenth-century France. Nerval and his contemporaries, moved by impossible longings for the infinite, paralysed by indecision, desired above all some spiritual certainty but could not find the way: 'L'homme matériel aspirait au bouquet de roses qui devait le régénérer par les mains de la belle Isis;[10] la déesse éternellement jeune et pure nous apparaissait dans les nuits, et nous faisait honte de nos heures de jour perdues'. The word *perdues* recalls the title Nerval intended to give to *Les Filles du Feu*: *Les Amours perdues*, and the title of the first chapter of *Sylvie*: 'Nuit perdue'. It means more than accidental loss: it implies something wasted, a vain effort, a misplaced hope, days lost in the pursuit of something less than the pure ideal incarnate in the goddess. Revolt was not at all what these young men had in mind. They thought in terms of 'renaissance', but vaguely, hesitantly; they turned their backs on public action and sought refuge in 'cette tour d'ivoire des poètes, où nous montions toujours plus haut pour nous isoler de la foule'. There they could breathe at last, 'ivres de poésie et d'amour'; but Nerval, writing in 1853, was clearly aware of the flaw in their diamond, of the distinction between the ideal and the terrestrial object to which the mind attaches it, between the goddess herself and the woman who only *appears* to be queen or goddess:

Amour, hélas! des formes vagues, des teintes roses et bleues, des fantômes métaphysiques! Vue de près, la femme réelle révoltait notre ingénuïte; il fallait qu'elle apparût reine ou déesse, et surtout n'en pas approcher.

He tells us in *Petits Châteaux de Bohême* that the daytime representative of his nightly dream of the Queen of Sheba was a beautiful singer: 'Cette dernière réalisait vivante mon rêve idéal et divin' (I, 71). In *Sylvie* he makes it plain that the essential condition of this *réalisation* is that the earthly embodiment of the ideal should not be 'vue de près'.[11] The quest for the ideal begins to look like a useless striving for the unattainable: for if, to avoid disappointment, one chooses illusion, one chooses also to be eternally unrequited: 'C'est une image que je poursuis, rien de plus'.

Tempted momentarily by a return of fortune to try to buy his ideal, the narrator in *Sylvie* resists the temptation, less, one feels, because he is unsure of success than because he would not really wish to succeed. His eye catches an announcement in the newspaper about the Fête du Bouquet which is due to take place the next day at Loisy in the Valois; he remembers the fête from his childhood. In bed, half-asleep, his mind runs over his memories of the Valois, the 'terre maternelle' he had already celebrated in *Angélique*. He recalls a château, a park, a group of young girls dancing, his companion Sylvie—'Je n'aimais qu'elle, je ne voyais qu'elle,—jusque-là!'—and Adrienne singing. We shift imperceptibly into the past; it is the château of 'Fantaisie': 'un château du temps de Henri IV avec ses toits pointus couverts d'ardoises et sa face rougeâtre aux encoignures dentelées de pierres jaunes'. A magical moonlight isolates the figure of Adrienne, and the children are silent: 'Nous pensions être en paradis'. For Adrienne the boy conceives at once 'un amour impossible et vague'; the following year, when he returns for the holidays, he learns that she is to become a nun. In a flash of insight the narrator, half-asleep, realises that his 'amour vague et sans espoir' for the actress is only the reflection, born of a physical resemblance, of his love for Adrienne, 'fleur de la nuit éclose à la pâle clarté de la lune, fantôme rose et blond glissant sur l'herbe verte à demi baignée de blanches vapeurs'.[12] For a brief moment he entertains the idea that they may be one and the same, so that Adrienne is now within his reach. He immediately rejects the idea, as he had already rejected the idea of approaching Aurélie: 'Aimer une

religieuse sous la forme d'une actrice! . . . et si c'était la même!—
Il y a de quoi devenir fou! . . . Reprenons pied sur le réel'.
Refusing to approach too closely to the 'image' in either form, he
turns to the 'réel', to Sylvie whom he has not seen for three years
(and here the narration slips imperceptibly into the present
tense): 'Elle existe, elle . . .' He sets off for the Valois, where the
villagers will be dancing all night, and thus he begins his travels
back into past time, under the sign of a motionless clock, and
without a watch: 'Quelle heure est-il? Je n'avais pas de montre'.
We are entering a timeless world; his Renaissance clock has not
been wound for two centuries, and is thus still marking the time
of 'Fantaisie': 'De deux cents ans mon âme rajeunit' (I, 18).
From this point, the story becomes increasingly dream-like, the
'real' increasingly difficult to pin down. During the journey, the
narrator recalls and describes a later period of his youth, when
after the fête the young people crossed a lake to picnic on an
island; the scene reminds him of Watteau's *Voyage à Cythère*. He
offers a garland of flowers to Sylvie, and she seems to forgive him
for his earlier infidelity. Next day he goes with Sylvie to visit her
aunt in the neighbouring village of Othys. They find in a trunk
the clothes which the old aunt and her husband, who is now dead,
had worn at their wedding. The children dress up as bride and
groom: 'nous étions l'époux et l'épouse pour tout un beau matin
d'été'.[13] We return abruptly to the present, and to the coach which
is now passing Châalis. The ruins of the abbey remind the
traveller of another point in time past, when he saw a mystery
play enacted in the abbey ruins, in which Adrienne appeared
dressed as a holy spirit with a flaming sword.[14] He begins suddenly to wonder whether he is imagining or has dreamed of
these things: 'Ce souvenir est une obsession peut-être!', and is
glad when the coach stops and he arrives at Loisy: 'j'échappe au
monde des rêveries'. We are back in present time.

He finds Sylvie, but she is a stranger, cool, self-possessed and
sensible; she tells him: 'les choses ne vont pas comme nous voulons
dans la vie'. He confesses to her that he has been obsessed with a
dream, and begs her to save him: but they are interrupted before
she can reply. The whole village retires to rest after the fête, but
the narrator is unable to sleep; it is now broad daylight. He
wanders sadly among the places he had known as a child, his

uncle's house, still furnished but empty, and Ermenonville where the empty park is growing wild. Returning to Loisy, he begins to realise that Sylvie has lost her simplicity. He takes her to Châalis, and there he makes her repeat after him the song which Adrienne had sung in the mystery play. It does not exorcise the ghost, and he is even further estranged from Sylvie. He too has lost his innocence: 'J'essayais de parler des choses que j'avais dans le cœur, mais, je ne sais pourquoi, je ne trouvais que des expressions vulgaires, ou bien tout à coup quelque phrase pompeuse de roman,—que Sylvie pouvait avoir lue. Je m'arrêtais alors . . .' He realises that his heart is not in it at all, and though he offers as excuse the fact that 'Sylvie, que j'avais vue grandir, était pour moi comme une sœur', it is clear that he would feel the same even if she were not 'quelque chose de sacré'; what really troubles him is the fact that he cannot sincerely offer her his love, and the idea of a loveless seduction appalls him: 'il y a des hommes qui jouent si bien la comédie de l'amour! Je n'ai jamais pu m'y faire, quoique sachant que certaines acceptent sciemment d'être trompées'. On their return to Loisy he learns that Sylvie is probably to marry a young man from the village. 'Sylvie m'échappait par ma faute . . .' He leaves the next morning for Paris. In the evening, back in the theatre, he sends an unsigned letter to the actress, and refusing to compete for her favours, sets off the next day for Germany. 'Qu'allais-je y faire? Essayer de remettre de l'ordre dans mes sentiments'. On his return, he makes himself known to Aurélie. The following summer, the company of actors to which she belongs travels to the Valois; the narrator goes with them as their *seigneur poète* (like Brisacier in the introduction to *Les Filles du Feu*). He takes Aurélie to the château where he had first seen Adrienne (the scene parallels his visit to Châalis with Sylvie); but she is unmoved. When he tells her the story of his obsession, her reply stuns him: 'Vous ne m'aimez pas! Vous attendez que je vous dise: "La comédienne est la même que la religieuse"; vous cherchez un drame, voilà tout, et le dénoûment vous échappe. Allez, je ne vous crois plus'. He realises at once that she is right:

Cette parole fut un éclair. Ces enthousiasmes bizarres que j'avais ressentis si longtemps, ces rêves, ces pleurs, ces désespoirs et ces tendresses . . . ce n'était donc pas l'amour? Mais où donc est-il?

Here the story breaks off, and the final chapter, 'Dernier Feuillet', tries to elicit the meaning of all the experiences which the narrator has been passing in review, and which, we suddenly realise, all belong to the past. He calls them *chimères*:

Telles sont les chimères qui charment et égarent au matin de la vie. J'ai essayé de les fixer sans beaucoup d'ordre, mais bien des cœurs me comprendront. Les illusions tombent l'une après l'autre, comme les écorces d'un fruit, et le fruit, c'est l'expérience. Sa saveur est amère; elle a pourtant quelque chose d'âcre qui fortifie . . .

Sometimes, he tells us, he visits Sylvie, her husband and her children. Watching their happiness, he reacts as he does in *Octavie*: 'Je me dis: "Là était le bonheur peut-être; cependant . . ." '—the *cependant* shows that though he now recognises his *chimères* for what they are, he is by no means convinced that the 'real' world is preferable. Like other incidents in the story, this one has its literary parallel, a wry one: 'Je l'appelle quelquefois Lolotte, et elle me trouve un peu de ressemblance avec Werther, moins les pistolets, qui ne sont plus de mode'. The implication, of course, is not that gentlemen no longer carry pistols, but that the idea of killing oneself for love is no longer acceptable—again, 'le dénoûment vous échappe', and one is reminded of Brisacier's observation: 'on ne se perce pas le cœur avec une épée de comédie . . . quand on est un héros de tragédie . . .' The grand gestures of novel and drama bear no relation to the helpless anguish of life itself, just as the 'phrase pompeuse de roman' cannot express true feelings of love or joy. Thus the final confrontation offers another lost *dénoûment*; the narrator takes Sylvie to see the actors during their tour, and asks her if she does not think Aurélie resembles Adrienne: 'Elle partit d'un grand éclat de rire en disant: "Quelle idée!" Puis, comme se le reprochant, elle reprit en soupirant: "Pauvre Adrienne! elle est morte au couvent de Saint-S . . ., vers 1832" '.

It is easy to slide over the surface of *Sylvie* and to see it as a charming romance. Yet there are hints of desperation that occasionally break the smooth flow of the narrative: 'Il y a de quoi devenir fou . . . un entraînement fatal . . . Ce souvenir est une obsession peut-être . . . "Sauvez-moi!" . . . Telles sont les chimères qui charment et égarent . . .' The reference to

Goethe's *Werther* shows that much was at stake, even if this story has apparently avoided catastrophe. What is the writer looking for in the timeless world of memory? Some clue, it would appear, to the mystery of his own bewildered affections, just as his journey to Germany was meant to 'remettre de l'ordre dans mes sentiments'. He loves Aurélie because he loved Adrienne. He loved Adrienne essentially because she was surrounded with a magical prestige compounded of her noble descent, the beauty of the night, her golden hair, her singing, and the fact that she was to become a nun. That is, he loved her because she was everything that his childhood companion, the real and accessible Sylvie, was not. Returning to Sylvie to escape his obsession, he tries to turn their relationship into something as steeped in poetry as the memory of Adrienne in the dusk. He adds music, folk-lore, Watteau, Rousseau, and the beauty of the landscape to reinforce this 'amitié tendre'. It is all to no avail; in the end he himself realises that he is 'talking like a book'. That is why he blames himself: 'Sylvie m'échappait par ma faute'. He was unable to accept her as she really was; running away from the image behind the footlights to the girl of whom he could say 'Elle existe, elle . . .', he makes the fatal mistake at Châalis of trying to turn Sylvie into Adrienne, of rejecting her present reality and using her as a link with that past whose empty monuments stand around him, yet which remains, in his mind, more alive than the present. He loses Aurélie (who had sufficient insight to question him 'Si c'est bien *pour moi* que vous m'aimez') for exactly the same reason.

He seems to have rejected reality in favour of the *chimère*. In point of fact it was hardly even a question of choosing, at this stage, between the real and the ideal. He had already chosen the ideal, and his approach to reality is fundamentally altered by that choice. He can only accept the Sylvie who forms a part of his memories of the Valois, memories in which she becomes confused with other girls, memories which are inevitably at one remove from reality and blended with images drawn from Rousseau or from Watteau. Unfortunately, reality has a will of its own. Sylvie rejects him ('il faut songer au solide'), and Aurélie insists that she wants to be loved '*pour moi*'; each of them prefers a more prosaic man who sees her as she is.

As well as the reference to 'les chimères qui charment et égarent' which links *Sylvie* to the sonnets of *Les Chimères*, the story touches more specifically at one point upon 'El Desdichado'. The existence of Sylvie is affirmed for the narrator by a vivid memory of her home: 'Je revois sa fenêtre où le pampre s'enlace au rosier'.[15] This vision surely contributes to the eighth line of 'El Desdichado': 'Et la treille où le pampre à la rose s'allie . . .' The vine- and rose-hung trellis may be the one which Nerval saw in the Vatican garden;[16] it is also the trellis by Sylvie's window. The reference adds a further dimension to our understanding both of 'El Desdichado' and of *Sylvie*. The darkness of the first quatrain of the sonnet, with its lost bright star, is the element of illusion, of Adrienne, 'fleur de la nuit'; the broad daylight of the second quatrain is the element of the real, of Sylvie, and of 'le bonheur peut-être', the possible rescue from 'la nuit du tombeau'. The opposition recurs in *Octavie*, where the mysterious embroideress belongs to the sulphurous night, and Octavie to the saving grace of daylight: yet she too is ultimately rejected.

The lesson of *Sylvie* is clearly drawn by the poet himself:

Ermenonville! . . . tu as perdu ta seule étoile, qui châtoyait pour moi d'un double éclat. Tour à tour bleue et rose comme l'astre trompeur d'Aldébaran, c'était Adrienne ou Sylvie,—c'étaient les deux moitiés d'un seul amour. L'une était l'idéal sublime, l'autre la douce réalité.

The opposition of *bleu* and *rose* repeats the association of Adrienne with night and of Sylvie with daylight. After the 'Voyage à Cythère', when the narrator decides to spend the night outdoors, he sees in the misty moonlight the walls of a convent and wonders if it is the one where Adrienne lives, but at dawn he dismisses the idea firmly: 'Le jour en grandissant chassa de ma pensée ce vain souvenir et n'y laissa plus que les traits rosés de Sylvie'. The ideal belongs to the moonlit night, and the real to the light of the sun. If nothing now remains of either, it is because he rejected the real in favour of the ideal; but the ideal (of which Adrienne, like Aurélie, was only an image) was always unattainable—indeed it is the essence of the ideal that it should be unattainable, since his 'seul amour' was the one he describes at the beginning of *Sylvie*: 'Amour, hélas! des formes vagues, des teintes roses et bleues, des fantômes métaphysiques!' The *chimère* may appear to find its embodiment, but the reality in which we think we see it, will inevitably prove to be flawed. How could it be otherwise, since the real object of the poet's striving is a union with something divine? For the spirit seeking such a consummation, union with mere humankind is at best only a poor reflection of imagined glory, at worst a disastrous mistake, almost a blasphemy. It is thus that in *Octavie* the poet reflects that 'le fantôme du bonheur n'avait été que le reproche d'un parjure'. The only hope for the spellbound seeker of the infinite is to learn to understand his own compulsions, to treat his human loves with kindness, and to direct his yearnings to their proper end. There is a hint, at the end of *Sylvie*, that Nerval has learned this lesson; that the tragic ending which is an essential part of Romantic love has proved, for him, to be unnecessary. When he came to complete *Aurélia*, he could spell out this lesson with the conviction of experience.

OCTAVIE

The shortest of the pieces in *Les Filles du Feu*, *Octavie* is by no means the least significant. The text has a curious and complicated history. The central episode appeared as early as 1842, among the letters published anonymously in *La Sylphide* under the title of 'Un Roman à faire'. It was published again separately, with the author's signature, in *L'Artiste* (1845), and was then called 'L'Illusion'—a title which links it at once with *Les Chimères*. In 1853 Nerval revised and expanded it, and it appeared in its present form (with minor variants) in *Le Mousquetaire* (17 December 1853), shortly after the publication in the same journal of 'El Desdichado'. Some further details were added to the text for publication in *Les Filles du Feu* (1854). It is not unlikely that the composition of both *Sylvie* and 'El Desdichado' is related to Nerval's re-reading of 'L'Illusion' in order to revise it, for there are important links between these three texts.

The additions made in 1853 are not merely attempts to extend an over-short text. They add certain details which are essential to a proper understanding of the central episode itself. The story begins in 1835; the author tears himself away from 'un petit théâtre' where he has been under the spell of 'une voix délicieuse, comme celle des sirènes'; he runs away to Italy. At Marseille he meets a young Englishwoman, who swims beside him in the sea. He is intrigued by 'cette fille des eaux, qui se nommait Octavie'; one day she catches a fish and gives it to him, and for a moment her mermaid-like image fuses with that of the 'sirène' he has left behind. Travelling overland, the writer makes his way to Rome, and to Civita-Vecchia where he intends to embark for Naples. The boat is delayed, and he visits the theatre in the evening; there he notices the English girl in a box, with her invalid father. The next morning he meets her on the deck of the boat, where in her impatience 'elle imprimait ses dents d'ivoire dans l'écorce d'un citron'—like the girl in 'Delfica'.[17] He approaches her and she seems half-pleased, half-annoyed by his attentions; but finally she offers to meet him the next day at Portici; at that moment they are crossing the bay of Naples 'entre Ischia et Nisida, inondées des feux de l'Orient'—one is reminded of 'Myrtho': 'ton front inondé des clartés d'Orient'. The writer spends the day wandering about Naples, and goes to the ballet in the evening, where he meets an old acquaintance, the Marquis Gargallo, who takes him home to meet his family. Emerging later with his head full of their 'discussion philosophique' (and perhaps equally dazed by the beauty of the marquise and her sisters), he cannot find his lodging. 'A force d'errer dans la ville, je devais y être enfin le héros de quelque aventure. La rencontre que je fis cette nuit-là est le sujet de la lettre suivante, que j'adressai plus tard à celle dont j'avais cru fuir l'amour fatal en m'éloignant de Paris'.

Here begins the text of 'Un Roman à faire', and of 'L'Illusion'. The letter belongs in time to a period after the incident at Naples ('plus tard'); but its new context has already warned us that the flight to Italy was in vain ('j'avais *cru* fuir'), so that we are not surprised to find that the tone of the letter links it at once with the time before the writer's departure from Paris; it is evident that he is still disturbed, still under a spell, still aware that in the long run he cannot be happy with this obsession, and aware now that it will not help to run away as he did before. The references at the beginning of *Octavie* to a theatre, and those in the letter to 'previous engagements' which the lady refuses to break at once, recall *Sylvie*, and Aurélie's insistence that 'il lui était difficile de rompre un attachement plus ancien'. A further addition to the text in 1854 (together with the phrase 'celle dont j'avais cru fuir l'amour fatal en m'éloignant de Paris') reinforces this aspect of the story: 'laissant à Paris un amour contrarié, auquel je voulais échapper par la distraction'. This phrase makes it clear that the writer regards his experiences in Italy as essentially an attempt to escape from an obsession; but the very first words of the letter tell us that he has not escaped. We know, therefore, before we read the account of the adventure in Naples, that it will not alter his situation.

The writer of the letter tells the woman he loves that he may be tempted, if she will not love him, to die for her. He wonders why he is preoccupied with death, 'comme s'il n'y avait que ma mort qui fût l'équivalent du bonheur que vous promettez'. Death seems to him not in the least frightening, but 'bonne et secourable', offering him 'le calme éternel'. He is then led to recall a previous occasion when death had appeared to him thus. There follows an account of his adventures in Naples on the night when he lost his way, which was, the letter tells us, three years before the time of writing. He met a young woman, 'une jeune femme qui vous ressemblait', and went with her to her home. There he deliberately engaged in self-deception, pretending that the young woman was the 'sirène' of the Paris theatre. The atmosphere is strange and hallucinatory. The description of the room, in which the writer saw 'quelque chose de mystique', lends credence to the power of 'la bizarre illusion que mon âme acceptait sans peine'. A statuette of the Madonna and an image of Sainte Rosalie 'couronnée de roses violettes' (recalling the 'rose au cœur violet' of 'Artémis'), introduce a note of mysticism; the walls, 'blanchis à la chaux', recall those of a monastic cell; there are paintings of ancient gods; and the room is full of rich stuffs which the girl embroiders for church vestments. But on a table is a 'Traité de la divination et des songes', which makes him think that she must be a sorceress, or at least a gipsy. The strange language which she speaks delights him, the strange jewels with which she decks herself dazzle him; she seems to him like an enchantress, 'une de ces magiciennes de Thessalie à qui l'on donnait son âme pour un rêve'.

In the morning he runs away from 'ce fantôme qui me séduisait et m'effrayait à la fois', and goes up to Posilipo where, he

says, he was tempted to throw himself into the sea. 'Je n'étais
pas attristé le moins du monde ... mais dans mon cœur il y
avait l'idée de la mort'. He has been made aware of the fact that
he is not loved. The caresses of the strange embroideress offered
him only 'le fantôme du bonheur'; the woman who obsesses him
is unaware of his existence; he has no hope of ever being loved,
and he is tempted to die. But he is afraid of damnation, he says;[18]
and besides, perhaps he may still achieve his goal. He prays to
God to give him 'la résolution, qui fait que les uns arrivent au
trône, les autres à la gloire, les autres à l'amour!' The effect of
this prayer is deeply ironical when one considers that at the
beginning of the letter, the writer has shown himself still to be
unsure whether he is, or ever will be loved—and still lacking in
resolution: 'J'ai été timide ... J'ai entouré mon amour de tant
de réserve, j'ai craint si fort de vous offenser ...'

At this point the letter ends. The text of *Le Mousquetaire* adds
a parenthesis (slightly adapted for *Les Filles du Feu*), beginning
'Je n'ai pas tout dit sur cette nuit étrange'. The phrase suggests
that Nerval was prepared, in 1853, to examine his experiences
more closely and to try to tell the whole truth—a suggestion which
is borne out by the publication, early in 1854, of *Les Chimères*. It
is not merely, however, that he has been concealing things from
the reader which he is now prepared to reveal. The evasion was
at a much deeper level. In writing *Sylvie*, Nerval set out to discover
the truth which had been half-hidden from himself, to uncover
the illusion and see it for what it was; it is probable that the
insights he gained in the process enabled him to complete *Octavie*
by analysing the central episode.

The passage added in 1853 describes how Vesuvius erupted
during the night, scattering ash over the town: 'une poussière
chaude et soufrée m'empêchait de respirer'. There is an obvious
link with 'Myrtho':

> Je sais pourquoi là-bas le volcan s'est rouvert ...
> C'est qu'hier tu l'avais touché d'un pied agile,
> Et de cendres soudain l'horizon s'est couvert.

In *Octavie*, the writer seems glad to leave his 'facile conquête',
and other texts reveal that the incident disturbed him profoundly.[19] There is a hint in *Octavie* that he felt guilty about his

adventure with the strange girl; in the final section, added in 1853, Nerval refers to 'cette nuit fatale où le fantôme du bonheur n'avait été que le reproche d'un parjure'.

After the description of the eruption of the volcano, the text of 1853 continues by recalling to the reader the appointment at Portici. It was that recollection, Nerval added in 1854, that banished all thought of death from his mind. There is another source here of the lines in 'El Desdichado':

> Dans la nuit du tombeau, toi qui m'as consolé,
> Rends-moi le Pausilippe et la mer d'Italie . . .

Octavie represents a normal, daylight world in contrast to the 'fantôme' of the previous night, just as Sylvie does in contrast to Adrienne, 'fleur de la nuit'.[20]

The writer meets Octavie at Portici and takes her to Pompeii. There, in the temple of Isis, he explains the mysteries to her, as he had learned them from Apuleius; they enact the rites, Octavie playing the rôle of Isis and Nerval that of Osiris. The reader is at once reminded of the scene at Châalis in which the young narrator makes Sylvie play the rôle in the mystery play which had been played by Adrienne, and after which he finds that he cannot approach her. The scene in *Octavie* is followed by a similar failure, due to a similar inhibition: in the presence of mystery, the terms of human affections seem empty and unworthy: 'frappé de la grandeur des idées que nous venions de soulever, je n'osais lui parler d'amour . . . je lui avouai que je ne me sentais plus digne d'elle'. He tells Octavie about the previous night's adventures and about his feeling that he has perpetrated 'un parjure'. The implication is that he has derogated once from his high ideal, and refuses to do so again. One cannot help surmising that in casting Octavie as the goddess Isis he was deliberately placing her beyond his reach. Moreover by allowing her to understand why he turned to her at all, he effectively alienates her, in the same way as he alienates both Sylvie and Aurélie.

The final paragraph, with a sudden jolt, replaces the episode in the time-scale which the narration has obscured. The writer, we are told, met Octavie again 'il y a dix ans'—which reminds us that the original meeting, and the subsequent writing of the letter, took place a long time ago. When he revisited Naples on his return from the Middle East, he saw Octavie with her husband, a painter who had become completely paralysed soon after their marriage, and who was intensely jealous of his wife, despite her devoted care (one is reminded of Isis's 'époux farouche' in 'Horus'). The story ends abruptly, on a note that recalls the ending of *Sylvie*: 'Le bateau qui me ramenait à Marseille emporta comme un rêve le souvenir de cette apparition chérie, et je me dis que peut-être j'avais laissé là le bonheur'.

Being earlier in date than *Sylvie*, to which it is obviously closely related, the 'letter' which forms the central section of *Octavie* does not thoroughly explore the implications of the experience it records. The same is true of 'Delfica', published in 1845, at the same time as the version of the letter to which Nerval gave the title of 'L'Illusion'. However, the sonnet 'Myrtho', which probably dates from the same period as 'Delfica' but remained unpublished, is more revealing; and the title 'L'Illusion' indicates that by 1845 Nerval was in no doubt as to the nature of the experience, even if he had not faced all its implications.[21] When he came to rework the text in 1853, he made the account at least as full as that in 'Myrtho', and the questions which the experience raises, for both writer and reader, are in fact answered, though only indirectly. In *Sylvie* the problem of illusion is explicitly discussed, and we can trace the growth of the poet's insight. By comparison, *Octavie* seems obscure; but it offers a valuable account of experience in the making, and of what it actually felt like to be caught between the real and the ideal.

CORILLA

Corilla (first published in *La Presse* in 1839, and reprinted with minor revisions in *Petits Châteaux de Bohême* in 1853) is a one-act play whose themes are evidently related to *Octavie* and to *Sylvie*. Fabio, a poet, is in love with Corilla, the prima donna of the San-Carlo opera house at Naples. Every evening, for three months, he has watched her from his seat in the theatre. He sends her letters and gifts by the hand of Mazetto, who works in the theatre. Mazetto arranges a brief meeting in the street; the lady tells Fabio that she will come that evening to the Villa-Reale (where Nerval met the embroideress in *Octavie*), but in disguise, for they must be discreet. Fabio discovers that his rival Marcelli has been dealing with Mazetto in exactly the same way, and is to meet Corilla at the same hour, but in a different place. Marcelli is confident, but Fabio dare not go to the Villa-Reale: he is sure that it is he who is being deceived. He sees Corilla with Marcelli and confronts them; Corilla tells him that she has never received his letters. Fabio, confused, tells her that he must have imagined their meeting: he admits that he has always been 'un triste rêveur'. He goes, and Corilla tells Marcelli to escort her to her home, and leave her. But Fabio returns suddenly, dragging Mazetto with him. Mazetto, forced to explain, argues that Marcelli wishes to marry Corilla (though he hints that her wealth may be a deciding factor), while Fabio loves only the brilliant figure behind the footlights. Mazetto thought therefore that Fabio would be content with believing that his letters were read; when he asked for a meeting, Mazetto found a flower-girl who resembled Corilla—it was she who spoke to Fabio, and it is she who now waits for him at the Villa-Reale. Marcelli bears Corilla away in triumph, advising Fabio to go and find the flower-girl: 'la nuée qu'embrassait Ixion valait bien pour lui la divinité dont elle était l'image, et je vous crois assez poète pour vous soucier peu des réalités'. Fabio is hurt because Corilla seemed unmoved at his discomfiture; he now feels that Marcelli is welcome to his 'conquête facile' (the phrase echoes the description of the embroideress in *Octavie*: 'ma facile conquête'). The flower-girl approaches; but though Fabio concedes her likeness to Corilla, he will not accept this reality in place of his vanished ideal—of which Corilla herself no longer seems a worthy incarnation: 'qui peut remplacer dans l'âme d'un amant la belle image qu'il s'est plu tous les jours à parer d'un nouveau prestige? Cella-là n'existe plus en réalité sur la terre; elle est gravée seulement au fond du cœur fidèle . . .'[22] Besides, he says, she has not Corilla's divine voice. The flower-girl begins to sing, and Fabio falls at her feet: she can be no other than Corilla herself. Marcelli arrives, sad because Corilla has dismissed him. He does not envy Fabio his inferior companion: 'Allons, faites-vous illusion à votre aise . . . Moi, je vais penser à la prima donna . . .' Corilla now admits that she has been testing both of them, and will not choose between them yet; for Fabio, she thinks, loves only the actress, not the woman, while Marcelli loves himself best of all. They all retire to supper.

The play tells us much about Nerval's view of love. Its Italianate intrigue is enriched by insights comparable to those in *Sylvie*. Corilla, like Aurélie, wants to be loved '*pour moi*', and recognises in Marcelli the ambitious *mondain*, in Fabio the idealistic dreamer. Mazetto judges that Fabio's love is 'de ceux qui viennent si fréquemment se brûler les ailes aux flammes de la rampe; passions d'écoliers et de poètes, comme nous en voyons tant . . .' Fabio demonstrates that Mazetto is right. He knows that he is only 'un triste rêveur'; he does not recognise Corilla without the footlights, and cares less that she does not want him than that she has spoiled his image of her. Moreover he is not really pleased at the idea of meeting her when the moment approaches:

Un mot d'elle va réaliser mon rêve, ou le faire envoler pour toujours! Ah! j'ai peur de risquer ici plus que je ne puis gagner; ma passion était grande et pure, et rasait le monde sans le toucher . . . la voici ramenée à la terre et contrainte à cheminer comme toutes les autres . . . je serais tenté de m'enfuir si elle ne m'avait aperçu déjà!

When Corilla agrees to meet him later, he becomes cross and sad, wonders whether she did not yield too easily, whether she was not influenced by the gifts he had sent her; he obviously thinks of her now as a 'conquête facile' (hence the alacrity with which he cedes her to Marcelli): yet Mazetto remarks to Corilla that 'tout Naples connaît l'austérité de votre vie'. Fabio misjudges reality because he has never really looked at it. In this he resembles the narrator in *Sylvie*: 'je n'avais pas encore songé à m'informer de ce qu'elle pouvait être . . .' Nor is he happy at the idea of living up to the letters and verses he has sent her. In *Aurélia* (I, 360–1) Nerval recounts a similar episode: a passionate letter to a woman he has met very recently finds the lady intrigued but sceptical: 'J'essayai de la convaincre; mais quoi que je voulusse lui dire, je ne pus ensuite retrouver dans nos entretiens le diapason de mon style . . .'

What is interesting is that *Corilla* was published as early as 1839, long before *Sylvie* and *Aurélia*. This suggests that Nerval had already understood and analysed the nature of theatrical illusion at that date—that is, at a time when according to the legend he was still completely infatuated with Jenny Colon. The lesson of *Corilla* makes it rather unlikely that most of the *Lettres à Aurélia* are anything but another examination of the same problem, on a more serious level: it would suppose a cynicism quite incompatible with everything we know about Nerval to suggest that with such insights, he could seriously lay siege to Jenny. Could he even, with such insights, allow himself for very long to worship her from afar? What makes the idea of a hopeless passion even less convincing is the fact, too often forgotten, that Nerval had a very healthy sense of humour: the tone of *Corilla* shows that he appreciated the ridiculous in Fabio as well as the pathetic. In *Les Nuits d'Octobre*, again, there is a good deal of self-mockery to counterbalance the romantic notions inspired by the Spanish dancer and the Venetian 'femme-mérinos'. The romantic illusion, it is constantly implied, does not survive in the cold light of day: it needs 'les feux de la rampe'.

JEMMY AND EMILIE

With the exception of *Isis*, the other pieces in *Les Filles du Feu* do not offer the same penetrating insights, but they are still related to the central theme despite their apparent difference.

The essay *Chansons et Légendes du Valois* is linked with both *Angélique* and *Sylvie*; we have already considered the importance of the folk-songs Nerval discusses in this essay, and of the very short story, *La Reine des Poissons*, which concludes it. It is typical of this poet that his very deepest concerns should be embodied thus in an apparently slight and impersonal text. In fact, all the texts in the volume have been chosen because they reflect some aspect of Nerval's experience. Even *Jemmy* and *Emilie*, sometimes excluded from editions of *Les Filles du Feu* on the grounds that Nerval did not write them,[23] have a logical place there (and after all, Nerval chose to put them in). *Jemmy* might be seen as an exploration of a situation like that of Nerval's own father: the predicament of a man who loses his wife and is left with a small son. It was perhaps this that attracted Nerval's attention to the German text by Charles Sealsfield of which *Jemmy* is a translation (see Note 29). Moreover, Jemmy's own situation also

recalls that of Dr Labrunie. The young man in *Jemmy* remarries
and creates a new home. When Jemmy escapes from the Indians
and returns, her child does not know her: 'le garçon s'effraya';
the incident is reminiscent of Nerval's account in *Promenades et
Souvenirs* of his father's return from the Russian campaign (I, 135):
frightened by the stranger's emotional embrace, Nerval cried
out 'Mon père, tu me fais mal'. Jemmy recognises that there is
no place for her in her old home, for the clock cannot now be turned
back; she returns to the Indians who have accepted her as one
of themselves. The image of her sorrowing husband and child,
which Jemmy nursed through five years of captivity and for
which she struggled alone across hundreds of miles of dangerous
territory, proves, when she arrives, to be an illusion.

Similar echoes of Nerval's preoccupations may be found in
Emilie, which dates, like *Corilla*, from 1839. Nerval said of this
story 'j'y tiens beaucoup' (Letter to Giraud; I, 1086), a fact
confirmed by Maquet, who thought the plan Nerval had given
him rather wild, but agreed to it nevertheless as Nerval was so
insistent.[24] The story offers a remarkably fresh examination of the
ethics of military life and of war. Nerval was deeply interested in
soldiering and frequently refers, in his letters to Dr Labrunie, to
the fact that his father had been a soldier. Like Vigny, he was
imbued in childhood with the military myth, and like him became
disillusioned in later life; *Emilie* is Nerval's *Servitude et Grandeur
Militaires*. The story also offers, in Wilhelm, another example of a
character whose life has been governed for many years by a goal
which proves to be an illusion. He has based his estimation of
himself, and his judgement of the French, on the belief that his
father's death in war was an act of murder, and that therefore
the soldier who killed him was a common murderer. Sebillotte[25]
surmises that the young Nerval regarded his father as responsible
for his mother's death during the Russian campaign, and it may
well be that the problem of responsibility in war, which is central
to *Emilie*, is what interested Nerval in this story. If that is so,
there may be an indication that Nerval regretted having thought
his father guilty, for Wilhelm is finally condemned. Faced with
the reality of Desroches, who calls him 'misérable fou . . . rêveur
cruel', Wilhelm sees that his belief had no foundation in truth,
but was merely the product of his own despair, and he cries

'j'avais tort'. It is too late; his illusion has brought tragedy to his sister and causes the death of Desroches.

Of all the pieces accepted as belonging in *Les Filles du Feu*, *Isis* has been least often related in any way to its companions. This text was first published in 1845.[26] It is sometimes noted that the goddess Isis appears in the sonnet 'Horus' and also in the first chapter of *Sylvie*; and the final passage of *Isis*, which expresses a syncretic view of religion, has been related to the fifth sonnet of 'Le Christ aux Oliviers', and to the words of the goddess in *Aurélia*: 'Je suis la même que Marie . . .' (I, 399). But even M. Cellier, who notes that *Isis* shares a Neapolitan décor with *Corilla* and *Octavie*, regards it as 'un article documentaire, un reportage';[27] while the editors of the Pléiade edition imply that its presence in what is otherwise a work of fiction is explained, as in the case of the play *Corilla*, by the fact that 'le titre en est un prénom féminin'.[28] If all this were true, it would imply that there is no real connection between *Isis* and its companions in this volume, and that Nerval included it simply in order to make up the weight of his book.

Such an argument implies rather a poor view of Nerval's artistic conscience, and of his taste, and there seems to be no good reason why we should not accept that he included *Isis* in *Les Filles du Feu* because it really belonged there. Nerval may not have made its relation to the other pieces in the volume explicit; but not only is *Isis* in its rightful place in this context, one might even go so far as to say that it provides a key to the meaning of the whole volume.

The essay is short; of its four sections, half of the first and the whole of the second are translated (without reference to the source) from a German text, an essay on the cults of Isis by C. A. Böttiger, while almost a quarter of the last section is adapted from Apuleius. Since N. Popa[29] discovered the source of these parts of the text, *Isis* has been taken even less seriously than before. What matters in the text, however, is precisely what Nerval added to his borrowed passages. He took from Böttiger a description of the ceremonies, beliefs and customs of the devotees of Isis and Osiris, not as they were during the earliest Egyptian dynasties but in their later development after the death of Alexander the Great, and at a time when the ancient cults were in conflict first with the decaying religion of the last Roman emperors, then with the growing influence of the Christian religion. Around Böttiger's rather dull text, Nerval weaves a meditation of his own. The essay begins with a deliberate step back into the past: 'Avant l'établissement du chemin de fer de Naples à Résina, une course à Pompéi était tout un voyage . . .'[30] The journey is undertaken in order to achieve an even greater step backwards in time:

souvent même on restait sur les lieux jusqu'au lendemain, afin de parcourir Pompéi pendant la nuit, à la clarté de la lune, et de se faire ainsi une illusion complète. Chacun pouvait supposer en effet que, remontant le cours des siècles, il se voyait tout à coup admis à parcourir les rues et les places de la ville endormie; la lune paisible convenait mieux peut-être que l'éclat du soleil à ces ruines . . .

We are back in the moonlight world of Adrienne, where the absence of the clear light of day allows one 'une illusion complète'. Nerval goes on to describe a recent attempt to create the same illusion in precisely reconstructed detail: the ambassador's fancy-dress party peoples the streets of Pompeii with living ghosts; in theatres and forum they imitate the actions of the former inhabitants of the town, and in the temple of Isis, at the setting of the sun, the ancient ceremonies are re-enacted. One is at once reminded of the scene in *Octavie* in which Nerval, with the help of the English girl, mimes the ancient ritual.

At this point Nerval makes the transition to Böttiger's text, describing the ritual. At the beginning of the third section he returns to his meditation. Passing through Naples on his way home from Egypt (he is referring to his journey in 1843), he revisited the temple of Isis, where he sat and watched the setting sun, and the moon rising over Vesuvius, 'ces deux astres qu'on avait longtemps adorés dans ce temple sous les noms d'Osiris et d'Isis'. Deeply moved, he considers the difficulty of religious belief in his time: the passage is closely related to that in *Sylvie* (I, 242) in which he describes his 'époque étrange'. In *Isis* he is tempted to reject reason altogether:[31]

Enfant d'un siècle sceptique plutôt qu'incrédule, flottant entre deux
éducations contraires . . . me verrais-je entraîné à tout croire, comme
nos pères les philosophes l'avaient été à tout nier?—Je songeais à ce
magnifique préambule des *Ruines* de Volney, qui fait apparaître le Génie
du passé sur les ruines de Palmyre, et qui n'emprunte à des inspirations
si hautes que la puissance de détruire pièce à pièce tout l'ensemble des
traditions religieuses du genre humain ! . . .

Si la chute successive des croyances conduisait à ce résultat, ne serait-il
pas plus consolant de tomber dans l'excès contraire et d'essayer de se
reprendre aux illusions du passé ?

In the final section of *Isis*, Nerval proposes that paganism, in its
last days, was more and more drawn to its origins, and tended
more and more to attempt to re-establish the unity which had
been broken by the scattered development, in different areas, of
the various elements of the original myths. The deity is 'cette
éternelle Nature', but has been known under different names:
Venus, Cybele, Ceres, or Isis, the most ancient of all. The goddess
describes herself (Nerval is here quoting Apuleius) as 'la mère de
la nature'. Nerval goes on to suggest cautiously that not only is
Catholicism related to the ancient cults because of the historical
links between them and early Christianity, but it has itself undergone an evolution similar to that of paganism in its last years: 'la
dévotion à la Vierge n'est-elle pas devenue une sorte de culte
exclusif?' Still treading warily, Nerval suggests that there are
essential likenesses between successive embodiments of the
Mother-goddess: Isis and Horus, Demeter and Bacchus (whose
name in the Eleusinian rites was Iacchus-Iesus), the Virgin and
her Child. He compares the resurrection-myths of these different
religions, noting the resemblance between the stories of Atys,
Osiris and Christ.[32] His intention, as he is at pains to point out,
is not to question the truth of Christianity, but to assert the truth
of all religions: 'n'est-il pas vrai qu'il faut réunir tous ces modes
divers d'une même idée, et que ce fut toujours une admirable
pensée théogonique de présenter à l'adoration des hommes une
Mère céleste dont l'enfant est l'espoir du monde?'

The final paragraph of *Isis* makes a vital distinction between
those particular elements of Christianity and of related religions
which Nerval has been discussing, and the body of their doctrine
as a whole. He supposes that these religions supplanted the cult

of the Olympian deities because the pantheon of Greek and Roman mythology was 'd'une beauté trop précise et trop nette . . . en un mot, trop bien conçu au point de vue des gens heureux . . . pour s'imposer longtemps au monde agité et souffrant'. The world turned instead to the 'religions du désespoir', in which the only ray of light is the cult of the Divine Mother and her suffering Child.

Nerval describes the Catholic world's devotion to the Virgin as a 'culte exclusif': it is what it excludes that is interesting. What Nerval does not say, though it clearly follows, is that the exclusive cult of the Mother-goddess, gentle and loving, implies some degree of rejection of God-the-Father, the stern, demanding deity whose forgiveness is won only at the cost of self-denial. The loving mother is a symbol of particular poignancy for Nerval. In a letter of good wishes written to Dr Blanche in 1854 on the day of his marriage (I, 1146), Nerval refers to the doctor's bride: 'Elle si courageuse, si bonne, si préoccupée des intérêts de votre maison et de la santé de tous, c'est vraiment celle que vous deviez choisir, car elle est un second médecin affectueux et doux qui tempère et affermit votre autorité nécessaire'. Such a protective influence was missing from the home of Dr Labrunie; small wonder that when Nerval saw the goddess Isis in his dreams she said to him: 'Je suis la même que Marie, la même que ta mère, la même aussi que sous toutes les formes tu as toujours aimée' (*Aurélia*; I, 399). In that phrase Nerval reveals the links between *Isis* and the other pieces in *Les Filles du Feu*. All the women he has ever loved were substitutes for the Mother-goddess. His dream was a dream of Isis, as indeed he tells us in *Sylvie*: but how then could any of her representatives be equal to his longings? When they failed him, as they were bound to do, his mind turned to the idea of death, as it did on Posilipo in *Octavie*, or in the references to Werther in *Sylvie*. As reason undermines faith, so the test of experience reveals the inaccessibility of the ideal: 'levant ton voile sacré, déesse de Saïs! le plus hardi de tes adeptes s'est-il donc trouvé face à face avec l'image de la Mort?'

When, at the beginning of the second part of *Aurélia* (I, 385), Nerval contemplates the idea of his own death, he is led to think of God, and asks himself: 'Pourquoi donc est-ce la première fois, depuis si longtemps, que je songe à *lui*?' He had indeed rejected

God-the-Father in his scheme of things, as Kneph is rejected in 'Horus', and Jehovah in 'Antéros'. One passage in *Isis* reveals that Nerval was obscurely aware, even as he wrote his panegyric to the Mother-goddess, that he was evading a problem: 'Il serait si beau d'absoudre et d'arracher aux malédictions éternelles les héros et les sages de l'antiquité!' To effect a total reconciliation between the old and the new gods, pardon must logically be extended to *all* things which human beings have called divine: reconciliation must include God-the-Father as well as the Mother-goddess and her Child. In *Les Filles du Feu* Nerval considers the *chimère* of woman's love, and correctly identifies it in his own case as a substitute for religious belief. In *Isis* he seems to be trying to transfer his metaphysical longings from the illusory figures of the daughters of fire to the goddess herself: but she is equally a subterfuge, too easily approached, too kind, bathed in that moonlight which is her element. Moonlight, which in the streets of Pompeii allows one 'une illusion complète' and which surrounds the magical image of Adrienne, is the antithesis of the sunlit world to which Sylvie belongs, and which is also the world of that God-the-Father whom the poet is trying to evade: for as he tells us in *Aurélia*, 'Dieu, c'est le soleil'.

Illusion, in all the pieces in *Les Filles du Feu*, is not a transitory error of vision, but a rarefied atmosphere which the dreamer breathes, through which he moves, until he is rudely awakened. The curious parenthesis in *Angélique*: 'les rêveurs succèdent aux hommes d'action', may well be a reference not merely to the gap between the heroic military Bucquoy and his visionary descendant, but also to the essential difference between Nerval and Dr Labrunie, whose exploits as an army doctor in the Napoleonic campaigns are several times mentioned in Nerval's letters to his father.[33] There seems at first to be little doubt which of the two Nerval would prefer to be. By following 'le rêveur', the narrator of *Angélique* is led from one delightful experience to another, and finally into his own world of dreams and memories; when for a moment he follows the 'homme d'action' by purchasing the book about the earlier Bucquoy, he immediately regrets it. This antithesis between action and dreams is repeated throughout *Les Filles du Feu*. Angélique's father, 'maréchal des camps et armées du roi', is an authoritarian man who runs his household like a military enterprise; Angélique is 'd'un caractère triste et rêveur'. Tord-Chêne is an energetic tyrant; his nephew and the Reine des Poissons seek refuge—and each other—'dans le rêve'. Marcelli is a practical man of action who teases Fabio about his lack of interest in 'les réalités' and advises him to cut his losses; Fabio is 'un triste rêveur'. Desroches is a gallant soldier; Wilhelm, 'miné par l'étude ou par les chagrins', withdraws from action and is called 'rêveur cruel'. Jemmy personifies both action and dreams, exchanging an obsession with the past for useful activity and relative contentment. Sylvain is 'un jeune homme qui a l'ambition de s'établir'; the narrator in *Sylvie*, lost in his memories, wonders if they are real, 'ou bien si je les ai rêvés', and reminds himself that 'c'est une image que je poursuis, rien de plus'. It should be noted that while the dreamers are more sympathetic than the men of action, they are also unhappy. Nerval was ambivalent about this, as about so many things, and makes his Adoniram remark contemptuously that 'Les hommes à paroles succèdent aux gens d'action' (II, 515); he sometimes rather envied the men of action, and his energies were devoted not only to pursuing his *chimère*, but also to learning to master it. The last pages of *Sylvie* show that the poet has understood the nature of his illusion, but cannot yet see where truth is to be found: 'ce n'était donc pas l'amour? Mais où donc est-il?' The answer, which lay in the total reconciliation which he imagined in *Isis* and which he thought would be 'si beau', could only come as the result of a further, more searching examination of his past experience: it will be found in *Aurélia*.

VI

LA PANDORA

Although Nerval finally withdrew *La Pandora* from *Les Filles du Feu*, it was originally intended to find its place there. The text of *La Pandora* is generally considered to be 'incoherent', if not 'delirious',[1] and thus among the most difficult of access of all Nerval's works. It is true that it does not display the same clear balance and the same limpidity of language as the pieces in *Les Filles du Feu*; yet even those have their darker side: the despair of Angélique, the obsession of Wilhelm, the temptation to suicide in *Octavie*, the cry 'Sauvez-moi' and the references to Werther in *Sylvie*. In *La Pandora* this element of darkness is predominant; but this does not mean that the text is incoherent. We must distinguish between the experiences of the writer and his controlled use of them: *La Pandora* is a perfectly lucid account of a nightmarish experience. As with *Les Chimères*, the difficulty arises from our expectations of a familiar logic. The narration in *La Pandora* follows the logic of nightmare vision, not that of waking speech; time and space, objects and people, are perceived in an extraordinarily vivid but fragmentary and inconsequential fashion, and if the narrator moves from one scene to another, he does not say why or how, but simply, as in dreams, appears in another place.

The epigraph, a quotation from *Faust*, sets the tone for the rest: 'Deux âmes, hélas! se partagent mon sein . . .' The duality is expressed in terms which parallel those in *Sylvie*: the love which is a fire ('*ardente* d'amour'), seeking an earthly form, a 'fille du feu', to which it may attach itself, moves constantly in darkness; metaphysical longing ('un mouvement surnaturel') moves the spirit out of darkness towards a heaven peopled by familiar souls.

Like the Brisacier episode, like *Sylvie*, *Octavie* and *Corilla*, the story of *La Pandora* begins by evoking a woman of the theatre, an actress or singer. The narrator's memories of her are 'cruels et doux', and his ambivalent feelings are matched by her mysterious ambiguity, which he stresses by describing her in the words of an enigmatic inscription: 'Ni homme, ni femme, ni androgyne . . .'[2]

The poet then sets the scene for the story of his love for Pandora:
the town is Vienna, 'rocher d'amour des paladins'; Vienna, he
says, comes under the sign not of the Holy Grail but of the sword
and the brotherhood of the sword: that is, if we borrow the terms
of *Angélique*, it belongs not to the *rêveurs* but to the *hommes d'action*.
But the poet is not one of this brave company: 'Je n'ai pu moi-
même planter le clou symbolique dans le tronc chargé de fer . . .'
He is a dreamer, offering Vienna 'mes plus douces larmes et les
plus pures effusions de mon cœur', singing his love songs in the
gardens of Schönbrunn where 'les chimères du vieux palais
m'ont ravi mon cœur pendant que j'admirais leurs yeux divins
et que j'espérais m'allaiter à leurs seins de marbre éclatant'. For
a moment he contrasts with this fantastic dream the memory of
a youthful love, and wanders in spirit by the woods, the fields,
and the ruined château which he passed on his way to see her.
It is the landscape of *Sylvie*; and as in *Sylvie*, he cries: 'je n'aimais
qu'*elle, alors*!'[3]

We jump at once from the remote and innocent past to winter
in Vienna. It is New Year's Eve, and Pandora is tormenting the
poet. Like all the encounters in this story, this scene acquires a
hallucinatory clarity through Nerval's technique of cutting
description to a minimum and giving to all actions the same
obsessive emphasis, to all dialogue the same anxious attention. With
his black coat and his timid air the narrator looks, says Pandora,
like a priest. He begs her not to mock him: 'ne plaisantons pas
avec l'amour, ni avec la religion, car c'est la même chose en
vérité'. Her reply is to insist on the game: 'Laissez-moi mon
illusion', she says. He replies bitterly that next time he will wear
a blue coat with gilded buttons that will give him an 'air cavalier';
she insists that she will refuse to see him without his black coat.
The incident seems a trivial one to recount at length, and there
is no attempt to explain its significance. Yet it is clear that the
poet's plea expresses a real agony of mind. The reason is not
hard to see: he is not by nature a man of action in a dashing blue
coat; he is a dreamer whose love is his religion. He realises in
helpless anguish (for how can he condemn her for behaving like
himself?) that he is being used as an element in someone else's
dream: he is the instrument of Pandora's 'illusion'; and worst of
all, through him she can perversely mock both love and religion.

She does not value his love, she values only the novelty of being wooed by a serious, timid lover: 'J'en ai bien assez . . . des attachés d'ambassade en bleu avec leurs boutons à couronnes . . . Ce petit-là me servira d'abbé'. If he wears his black coat, he may call for her next day in a carriage. He is filled with despair: he has no money. He goes to borrow from a friend (Alexandre Weill). As long as his friend's mistress Rosa (another actress) is in the room, the poet is met with refusal; then his friend escorts him to the door, and slips some money into his hand, explaining: 'J'ai sauvé ceci des mains de Dalilah . . .' Later, a girl called Kathi comes to see the poet in his room; he asks her to give him the flower she is wearing; she offers to sell it to him, and when he pretends not to understand, she becomes angry and leaves him, saying that her 'vieux baron' will give her better presents. He dines in an inn, then walks through the crowded streets where the brilliant shops are full of New Year gifts (he notices especially expensive toys from Nuremberg). He goes into a beer-cellar; here he is tempted to kiss the waitress, but remembers (in an echo of *Octavie*) 'le rendez-vous du lendemain'; after further wanderings he arrives at the embassy where he is to take part in charades (another theatrical ritual, like those involving the narrator with Sylvie or Octavie, and Fabio with Corilla). The whole of this section is written in a rapid, allusive style, but its meaning is surely clear: there is only one way to obtain the love that Pandora offers, and that is to buy it; she is no better than Rosa or Kathi, though not so open. The poet may try to see her as an ideal of something higher (it is that illusion which prevents him from succumbing to the charms of the waitress); but he realises that he will not be able to approach his ideal without money. One remembers Fabio in *Corilla*: 'le rayon qui fait vivre pour moi cette idole adorée est de ceux que Jupiter versait au sein de Danaé!' (I, 307). One remembers also the narrator in *Sylvie*, refusing to buy his ideal: 'je ne serai pas un corrupteur' (I, 244). The poet in *La Pandora* has admitted that it is not he who is corrupt, but 'l'artificieuse Pandora'.

The second part of *La Pandora* begins with an explanation of the context of the piece which links it with the account, in *Voyage en Orient*, of Nerval's visit to Vienna.[4] The text then continues with a sudden violent action: 'De colère je renversai le paravent

'. . . Je m'enfuis du salon à toutes jambes . . .' (presumably the salon of the embassy). Back in the beer-cellar the poet writes a letter: 'j'écrivis à la déesse . . . Je lui rappelais les souffrances de Prométhée, quand il mit au jour une créature aussi dépravée qu'elle . . .' That night, he sleeps badly. He dreams of the insolent beauty of Pandora, who appears with silver horns (a real *déesse*: it is the ancient form of the goddess Isis); he tames her by boldly grasping her horns. She becomes the Empress Catherine and offers him gifts of land and titles; but he is terrified:

'Malheureuse! lui dis-je, nous sommes perdus par ta faute—et le monde va finir! Ne sens-tu pas qu'on ne peut plus respirer ici? L'air est infecté de tes poisons, et la dernière bougie qui nous éclaire encore tremble et pâlit déjà au souffle impur de nos haleines . . . De l'air! de l'air! Nous périssons! . . .'

The choking sensations he records recur in the next episode, where they are caused by 'quelques pépins de grenade' (a well-known sexual symbol);[5] they recall the effects of the eruption of the volcano in *Octavie* (I, 290): 'une poussière chaude et soufrée m'empêchait de respirer', and the dream in *Les Nuits d'Octobre* where a similar difficulty in breathing ('il respire avec peine') accompanies distressing dreams after the poet has been fascinated by another 'femme à cornes': 'la femme aux cheveux de mérinos' (I, 105–6, 110). He finds himself suddenly in the Vatican gardens, where 'la belle Impéria' sits among the cardinals (an echo perhaps of Pandora's taste for priests?). At the sight of the gold dishes on the table he is moved to defy her, and to make it plain that he is not deceived: 'Je te reconnais bien, Jésabel!' He is at once swimming in a tropic sea, to be cast on the shore of Tahiti, 'l'île des Amours'.[6] There he is greeted and succoured by three girls who do not speak to him: 'Elles avaient oublié la langue des hommes'. He smiles and greets them: 'Salut, mes sœurs du ciel': he is in heaven at last, among familiar and friendly souls.

The dreamer awakes; it is daylight. At midday he goes to accompany Pandora to the Prater, anxious to see what effect his letter has had. While he is waiting for her to dress, a prince arrives who is evidently a rival. A farcical scene ensues, each refusing to give way to the other, while the prince (another man of action) alludes meaningly to his skill with sword and rapier.

Finally both accompany Pandora to the Kohlmarkt; the poet then goes with her to her music-shop, and to her dressmaker, where he waits for her. She emerges an hour later, in a bad temper, and orders him to take her home. In his rooms, he gives way to despair. Next morning he receives an invitation to another evening of charades, where he will no doubt meet Pandora again; refusing further humiliation, he leaves at once for Salzburg.

There is a postscript. The next winter, in a cold northern capital (Brussels), he meets Pandora again; but again he runs way from her.[7] She calls after him a final taunt, reminding him that it is again New Year's Eve: 'Où as-tu caché le feu du ciel que tu dérobas à Jupiter?' It is her reply to his letter: he may give her Prometheus's celestial fire as a New Year's gift—she values it no higher. The story ends on a solemn note:

Je ne voulus pas répondre: le nom de Prométhée me déplaît toujours singulièrement, car je sens encore à mon flanc le bec éternel du vautour dont Alcide m'a délivré.

O Jupiter! quand finira mon supplice?

'Je sens *encore* . . .': that is, at the time of writing *La Pandora*. The poet has still not been delivered from torment, though he may appear to be free. He knows now, however, that the problem does not lie between himself and a treacherous woman; it lies between himself and Jupiter.

Despite its discontinuity (which perfectly conveys the anguish behind the art), *La Pandora* is not difficult to understand. The actress Pandora is the other side of the idealistic coin which Nerval describes in *Corilla* and in *Sylvie*. She lures him like a siren and then refuses him: Pandora speaks only too well 'la langue des hommes'. The poet bitterly resents the power she wields: 'nous sommes perdus par ta faute . . .'; and finally he chooses to flee. Her last attempt to enslave him is cynical in the extreme: in exchange for his celestial fire she offers him a New Year's gift of her own: it is a box of those gaudy Nuremberg toys which he saw in the shops in Vienna.[8] Pandora is all the things that Fabio fears Corilla might be, and that the narrator in *Sylvie* half-fears that Aurélie might be.

The tragedy is not that women are false, but that they slight a genuine passion; they prefer 'la comédie de l'amour', of which, as he tells us in *Sylvie*, Nerval was incapable. Like the enchantresses to whom Nerval compares the embroideress in *Octavie*, they offer a dream, and take one's soul in exchange. So do the *chimères* of Schönbrunn: love them, and they will take away your heart; but they themselves are marble. The disillusion is that same agony that Nerval understood in Heine's *Intermezzo* (O.C. I, 89): 'La femme est la chimère de l'homme, ou son démon, comme vous voudrez,—un monstre adorable, mais un monstre . . .' In *Les Filles de Feu*, Nerval recounts his long flirtation with this creature of illusion; in *La Pandora* he paints her at her worst. What is most interesting about *La Pandora*, however, is that it points the way to the solution which *Aurélia* will find, by indicating that the true source of the poet's agony is his Promethean struggle with the deity, his inability to come to terms with God-the-Father and seek his salvation in Him, rather than in the *chimère* of woman's love. Nerval was justified in thinking that *La Pandora* should not be included in *Les Filles du Feu*. It would disturb what Nerval called 'le sentiment doux du livre': not however because it is any less lucid than the other pieces, but, on the contrary, because it speaks too clearly.

AURÉLIA

Nerval's *Aurélia* is a work of unusual density; there is scarcely a line in it which does not add significantly to the exposition of his theme. It differs from most of his other prose works in that it is frankly autobiographical, being presented as a non-fictional and analytical account of experiences undergone by the author. We have only to compare it with *Sylvie*, for instance, to see that Nerval's concern in *Aurélia* is primarily not with that special kind of structured truth which derives from the insights of art, but with simple truthfulness or honesty. Given his tendency (which he recognised himself) to view his life 'comme un roman', this second kind of truth must have been hard for him to attain. He succeeds by a scrupulous documentation, recording everything as it happened, and denying himself the artist's privilege of selecting and highlighting certain aspects of experience, of rejecting or minimising others. Despite his previous fears of seeming abnormal, he appears to hide nothing: the only omissions are details which would enable the reader to identify the people involved in his story. This is not only due to discretion. He also wishes to suggest that he is not unique; as he says himself (not for the first time): 'Peu importent les circonstances . . . Chacun peut chercher dans ses souvenirs . . .'[1] The essential problems which he faced are, he believed, the problems of every man. This belief inevitably makes of *Aurélia* something other than a clinical case-history. By accepting that he is representative and not unique, Nerval has given to his experiences the allegorical force of a Pilgrim's Progress, so that the banal acquires the poetic resonance of a myth (as it frequently does in *Les Chimères*). Moreover his analysis of his struggles is coloured to some degree by his instinctive refusal of the idea that they might be meaningless.

An initial difficulty in reading *Aurélia* stems from the subject itself: confronted by discussion of dreams, hallucinations, and spiritual uncertainties, the reader may be tempted to assume that *Aurélia* is fundamentally incoherent, and that its many

repetitions are merely helplessly obsessive restatements of themes
which Nerval had already employed in *Les Chimères, Les Filles
du Feu*, and the tales from *Voyage en Orient*. Such a view would be
incompatible with what Nerval himself has to say about this
work. Reaching a point in his narrative at which he knows he
must begin to record hallucinatory experiences whose logical
interdependence will not be obvious (indeed, he is himself not
altogether sure of it), he remarks (I, 364):

Si je ne pensais que la mission d'un écrivain est d'analyser sincèrement
ce qu'il éprouve dans les graves circonstances de la vie, et si je ne me
proposais un but que je crois utile, je m'arrêterais ici, et je n'essayerais
pas de décrire ce que j'éprouvai ensuite dans une série de visions insensées
peut-être, ou vulgairement maladives . . .

The word *analyser* suggests at once that in *Aurélia* we have an
attempt not merely to record but above all to make sense of the
poet's experiences. We have already observed that even *La
Pandora*, generally regarded as incoherent in structure, can be
seen to develop according to a logic of its own. It is the logic of
dream, which also determines the structure of 'Artémis'. The
dream-world is described in *Aurélia* as 'une vie nouvelle . . .
affranchie des conditions du temps et de l'espace, et pareille sans
doute à celle qui nous attend après la mort': the logic of dream
is the logic of eternity, not that of our everyday existence.[2] In
La Pandora, the poet under stress records as accurately as possible
his sensations and his reactions to his experiences, including his
dreams, but he is not sufficiently in control of his emotions to
attempt to explain them. In *Aurélia* the attempt is made, but it is
undertaken in all humility, for this poet is no self-assured *voyant*,
and is ready to concede the possibility that his visions may appear
to others to be 'insensées peut-être . . .'

Nerval was very well aware of the unique character of the book
he was struggling to write and of the dangers inherent in the
material he was manipulating. The apparent detachment of
the narration represents a supreme victory for the artist in
Nerval, for he was surely not detached: the subject of *Aurélia* is
no less than his own spiritual salvation, and it was of the greatest
importance to him that he should succeed in ordering the confusions he had lived through. This effort of understanding goes

hand in hand with a desire to produce a work of some moral value, a record which might be of help to others: 'je croirai avoir fait quelque chose de bon et d'utile en énonçant naïvement la succession des idées par lesquelles j'ai retrouvé le repos et une force nouvelle à opposer aux malheurs futurs de la vie' (I, 394). He wanted to explain and justify his career (that is, his whole life) both directly by discovering its moral significance, and indirectly by producing a work which would be its own justification. Aesthetic considerations were secondary, and in any case, as we have seen, aesthetic excellence is to be gauged, according to Nerval, by the extent to which the artist has succeeded in giving full and appropriate expression to his thought.

It was, in this instance, an extremely difficult task, not only because of the need for a vigilant objectivity, but also because Nerval was by nature a modest and a reticent man. The modesty is dignified and genuine, the product of that insight which led him to minimise the details peculiar to his own situation and to stress that he is much like any other man. The reticence was a more difficult barrier: it was composed partly of discretion and fear, partly of a distaste for public exhibition of his feelings, and not least because such exhibition can so easily lead to falsity and posturing. He had pleaded modesty, discretion and reticence in *Voyage en Orient* when refusing to speak of his experiences in Vienna: 'Mais . . . il me semble que vais te raconter l'aventure la plus commune du monde . . . et, pour ce que j'aurais à dire encore, je me suis rappelé à temps le vers de Klopstock: "Ici la Discrétion me fait signe avec son doigt d'airain." ' (II, 64); 'Je n'ajouterai pas un mot de plus, quant à présent. J'ai la pudeur de la souffrance, comme l'animal blessé qui se retire dans la solitude pour y souffrir longtemps ou pour y succomber sans plainte' (II, 93). As for the dangers of public discussions of emotion, he is quite explicit on this point in 'Les Confidences de Nicolas': 'Nous ne vivons pas, nous! nous analysons la vie! . . . Sais-tu ce que nous faisons, nous autres, de nos amours? . . . Nous en faisons des livres pour gagner notre vie' (II, 1072).[3] Nothing, he knew, is more difficult for the professional writer of fiction than to tell the truth 'naïvement'.

Beyond all these difficulties, there lay the further, inescapable difficulty of composing his text so as to reconstruct as exactly as possible the experiences he wished to consider. The final complexity of his narrative corresponds to the complexity of those experiences, and in fact the most fruitful approach to *Aurélia*, as to *Les Chimères*, is through the structure of the text. The pattern of the narration in *Aurélia* is chronological, but it shows a complex symmetry quite unlike the linear development usually associated with chronological narrative. Each major incident is paralleled in the course of time by one or more incidents of a similar kind, often calling forth an almost identical pattern of words from the poet. Since he constantly pauses to discuss the events which he recounts, repetition of an event leads to repetition of the discussion also. This recurrence of incident and idea is largely responsible for the apparent impenetrability of *Aurélia*: although in fact the discussion does lead the poet towards a constantly deepening understanding, it does so by infinitesimally small degrees, and superficially the text does not appear to make progress, but rather to be constantly arriving at a point which it has just left. Thus the reader may feel that he is observing a repetitive ritual which must surely have a meaning but which remains mysterious to the uninitiated. It may be that it was this apparent inconclusiveness which led Gautier and Houssaye to suggest that *Aurélia* was unfinished.[4]

The poet begins by speaking of dream, which he sees as a continuation and extension of waking life: 'une seconde vie . . . où le *moi*, sous une autre forme, continue l'œuvre de l'existence' (I, 359). The poet's conception of dream includes daydreams or waking visions as well as dreams in sleep; indeed all kinds of consciousness shade imperceptibly into each other. He clearly sees dream as a source of knowledge. As he remarks in *Voyage en Orient* (II, 108): 'Il est certain que le sommeil est une autre vie dont il faut tenir compte'. From dreams one can learn about one's own self, and about human nature in general; poets and thinkers who have recounted their dreams were offering us their 'études de l'âme humaine' (I, 359). Dreams are also a key to knowledge of the universe, for they put the dreamer in touch with 'le monde des Esprits', and are peopled by 'les pâles figures . . . qui habitent le séjour des limbes'. This sentence recalls Nerval's description, in the Preface to the 1840 edition of his translation of *Faust*, of a region in space where human souls 'conservent une forme perceptible aux regards des autres âmes, et de celles mêmes qui ne se dégagent des liens terrestres que pour un instant, par le rêve . . .'; these souls are 'les ombres . . . qui, chrétiennes ou païennes, mais non damnées, flottent au loin dans l'espace, protégées contre le néant par la puissance du souvenir' (O.C. I, 17–18).[5]

The poet's intention, he tells us, is to transcribe the dreams and visions he experienced during an illness, in what he calls 'l'épanchement du songe dans la vie réelle' (I, 363). He is insistent that this 'double' life does not lack coherence, even if it does not seem to conform to everyday notions of logic; he had made the same point in the introduction to *Les Filles du Feu*: 'Quelque jour j'écrirai l'histoire de cette "descente aux enfers", et vous verrez qu'elle n'a pas été entièrement dépourvue de raisonnement si elle a toujours manqué de raison' (I, 158).[6]

Nerval observes two phases in the development of the experience as a whole, and it is important to note that these do not correspond with the two parts of *Aurélia*: the first phase extends to the end of Chapter VIII of the *Première Partie*, and the second occupies the last two chapters of this part and the whole of the *Seconde Partie*. Whatever the reason for dividing the text into two parts (and we will consider this in due course), Nerval clearly sees the second phase of his illness as a continuation of the first: 'une rechute qui renoua la série interrompue de ces étranges rêveries' (I, 379). Despite the lapse of a considerable period of time, he recognised that the later experiences were essentially the same as the earlier ones, and his accounts of the two 'phases' show important similarities.[7]

The first phase is characterised by a regular pattern of alternating moods.[8] These moods appear to depend on fortuitous signs, dreams or visions which the poet interprets as having a threatening or a consoling nature. His interpretations may appear capricious, but there is in fact a logical sequence: time after time, the confidence inspired by a hopeful sign leads shortly to a sense of having been presumptuous, thence to fear, and rapidly to discouragement and distress. The poet expects to be punished for his presumption, and feels deeply guilty not only because of what he has just done, but for having committed all the wrong actions which he can recall from the past, and which appear to him with terrifying clarity. It seems to him that he is beyond redemption. At the lowest depth of despair, the slightest favourable sign appears like a gift from heaven itself—and the cycle begins again.

This basic pattern appears in the first few pages of the book. The poet begins by explaining that he had lost the love of a woman whom he calls Aurélia. He saw his rejection as the punishment for an unpardonable crime, which he does not specify. He contemplated suicide, but chose instead the distraction of 'les enivrements vulgaires', recognising the folly of taking too literally the ideals of poets, of trying to make a Laura or a Beatrice out of 'une personne ordinaire de notre siècle'. Later, he met Aurélia again and felt that she had forgiven him; he saw in her forgiveness 'quelque chose de la religion' which gave his hitherto profane love 'le caractère de l'éternité'. His joy in this revelation leads to a perilous overexcitement and confusion, so that unconnected incidents rapidly group together in his imagination to form a presage of his death. That is, he has finally been tempted to idealise the woman he loves, seeing her as the mediator of his redemption, and consequently feels presumptuous and deserving of punishment. A dream confirms his fear: he is in his school, and seems happy to linger there; after a while he leaves it for 'une sorte d'hôtellerie . . . pleine de voyageurs affairés', which seems to represent the adult world; here he loses his way among vast staircases and long corridors[9] and is terrified by the plunge to destruction of a huge winged creature which tries and fails to escape beyond the heavy clouds massed over the central court.[10] The following evening, at the appointed hour, he goes to meet his destiny, in a state of exaltation and convinced that he now understands 'les mystères du monde'; he believes that he will find those he loves in an eastern star whose brightness seems to draw him on. A friend tries to dissuade him; to Nerval he seems to take on the appearance of an apostle, and the poet, continuing on his way, rejects him and his God: 'je n'appartiens pas à ton ciel'. At the last moment he is seized by 'le regret de la terre et de ceux que j'y aimais'—at which point he is arrested. At the guard post he remains in a state of ecstasy, and sees a vision of a splendid but elusive goddess. But soon he feels that he is accompanied by another self, and remembers with fear the old

German tradition of the Doppelgänger: when a man sees his double, his death is near. He becomes depressed, and at the same hour of the following evening collapses and is taken to a clinic.

The dreams he next recounts repeat more or less exactly the sequence thus far, but are more detailed, and the poet now seems able to attempt an interpretation of them. He returns once more to a childhood scene, to 'une demeure connue'; it is the house with green shutters which he describes in *Sylvie* as 'la maison de mon oncle' (I, 260). He is welcomed by an old servant 'qu'il me semblait connaître depuis l'enfance'. The soul of his uncle speaks to him through a bird, telling him of his family; the living and the dead seem to exist simultaneously, and among them he includes a woman whose portrait hangs on the wall: she wears German costume, and though he does not say so, she seems to be the poet's mother, whom he always associated with Germany, where she died; certainly the house, 'sur les bords du Rhin', is that of 'un oncle maternel'. Passing through the centre of the globe, carried along veins of molten metal composed of human souls, he finds himself among brilliant islands, lit by a 'jour sans soleil', and is cast on a shore where an old man, his uncle, greets him.[11] He is in the Valois, 'où mes parents avaient vécu et où se trouvent leurs tombes'. There, tenderly greeted by his family, he is instructed by his uncle: he sees a vision of his family as 'une chaîne non interrompue d'hommes et de femmes en qui j'étais et qui étaient moi-même', and he feels that this is a representation in little of 'l'harmonie générale'. He is overjoyed at the notion of being reunited with his family for ever, but his uncle warns him that he still belongs to the material world, and that though matter cannot die, 'elle peut se modifier selon le bien et selon le mal'. Almost at once the poet is filled with fear and wonders if he is touching forbidden mysteries.

Next he finds himself in a hill-town, where he observes a race of men more vigorous than the rest, preserving their independence in the midst of a degenerate population. He is guided up stone-stepped streets to the highest reaches of the town, an enchanted place which recalls his description, in *Promenades et Souvenirs*, of Pontoise, remembered from his childhood: 'une de ces villes, situées sur des hauteurs, qui me plaisent par leur aspect patriarcal . . . et la conservation de certaines mœurs, qu'on ne rencontre plus ailleurs . . . les rues, en escaliers, sont amusantes à parcourir . . . on envie tout ce petit monde paisible qui vit à part dans ses vieilles maisons . . . au milieu de ces beaux aspects et de cet air pur . . .'(I, 140). In Pontoise he sought 'mon enfance et le souvenir de mes parents'; he finds them in his dream, where the inhabitants of the mountain heights are 'simples de mœurs, aimants et justes' (these words are repeated within a few sentences),[12] 'conservant les vertus naturelles des premiers jours du monde' (I, 370). As he is about to enter one of the rooms, a mysterious figure, a man robed in white, threatens him, and he wonders again if he is entering forbidden territory. He feels at home and happy among the people of the city, who are all 'vêtus de blanc', and especially with the young girls and children, who seem to constitute 'une famille primitive et céleste', and for whom he feels 'une sorte d'amour sans préférence et sans désir, résumant tous les enivrements des passions vagues de la jeunesse'.[13] The same overwhelming nostalgia is aroused by 'tous ces blancs fantômes de la jeunesse' in *Le Marquis de Fayolle* (I, 612); but even in his dream his delighted recognition of the pure love he finds in this 'paradis perdu' is overshadowed by the realisation that he must return to the real world, as his uncle had warned him.

In the real world he finds little sympathy with his visions, but one of his friends listens intently and exclaims 'N'est-ce pas vrai qu'il y a un Dieu?' The poet too sees his vision as a proof of the immortality of the soul and of the 'existence éternelle' of those he loves.[14] A further dream begins by confirming this idea, but it does not lead to the same confirmation of the existence of God. He is again in the family house; three women who symbolise for him 'des parentes et des amies de ma jeunesse' sit working in a room which seems more splendid than his memory of it; one of them speaks in a voice he remembers from his childhood; he is clothed in a gossamer stuff woven by their 'doigts de fée',[15] and feels like a small child. One of the women leads him into the garden. He follows her through a long arcade of trellis hung with grapes. Beyond it the garden has grown wild, the trees are smothered in vigorous creepers and the fruit hangs unpicked on the branches; long neglected, the garden barely shows the trace of its former paths 'qui l'avaient jadis coupé en croix'. Among the clumps of trees he sees statues 'noircies par le temps', and a spring of water tumbles from ivy-covered rocks into a lily pool. These images suggest to the reader (though not, as yet, to the poet) the abandoned faith of his childhood, his neglect of 'the way of the Cross' and its 'source d'eau vive'. The woman he is following holds in her arm a branch of *rose trémière* (the flower of 'Artémis'); the poet's description of her movement 'qui faisait miroiter les plis de sa robe en taffetas changeant' recalls the goddess in *Isis* (I, 300): 'sa robe aux reflets indécis passe, selon le mouvement de ses plis, de la blancheur la plus pure au jaune de safran . . .' The goddess begins to grow, till the whole garden is absorbed into her form and her face fills the sky; in growing thus she vanishes. The poet is frightened, and begs the goddess not to disappear, 'car la nature meurt avec toi'. He fights his way towards her fading image through thorns that stretch across his path, and stumbles on a heap of fallen stones. The garden has become a cemetery, and at the poet's feet lies the bust of a woman, which he recognises; he hears voices proclaiming that 'L'Univers est dans la nuit!'

The poet is unable to interpret this dream, and hints that its meaning, which he understood only later, was connected with the death of Aurélia. To the reader this appears inadequate as an explanation, and it seems likely that the poet's later 'understanding' was a mere rationalisation. At the time when he learned that Aurélia was dying, the poet remarks, he was not much distressed, since he had now a confirmed belief in immortality and was sure that he would meet her again; he reflected that she belonged to him in death more than in life. He was, he tells us, to pay dearly for that 'égoïste pensée', that is, again, for his presumption.

The clinic, with its hill-top situation, its trees, its 'air pur', and its 'société toute sympathique', resembles the city of his dreams;[16] here he is gradually restored to a calmer mood. He tries to fix in colour or clay the image of Aurélia 'sous les traits d'une divinité' —the goddess of his visions. He embarks on a history of creation, which he now recounts at length. He sees a constant alternation between periods of peace and harmony and periods of struggle and distress, the Deluge followed by the new world, the power of evil always ready to strike. These images obsessed him 'tour à tour', he says; and the duality of his vision, its darker side dominated by 'l'image souffrante de la Mère éternelle' (I, 379), clearly echoes his own vacillating moods. But his new interest in the history of creation indicates that he has now moved from an obsession with his personal 'paradis perdu' to a consideration of the alternating fortunes of the universe, and a search for that 'harmonie générale' which he had glimpsed in an earlier dream.

Here begins the account of the 'second phase' of his illness, and essentially it repeats, many years later, the pattern which we have already seen enacted twice. The acute stage of his illness is precipitated by a series of events similar to those which he recounts at the beginning of the first phase; but since the poet remembers the pattern of earlier events, one such event is now enough to make him anticipate the recurrence of the whole series. This time, 'préoccupé d'un travail qui se rattachait aux idées religieuses' (the conjunction is surely not fortuitous), he is struck by a sequence of apparently sinister signs which remind him at once of his earlier visions, and he falls heavily while descending a staircase.[17] He believes again that he is about to die, and again he welcomes the idea of death, until it occurs to him that he is unworthy of being reunited in death with Aurélia, because he has insulted her memory with 'de faciles amours'; the feelings of guilt are exactly like those aroused in the first phase by 'les enivrements vulgaires', and indicate that he still regards her as semi-divine. But the development of the second phase of his illness does not simply duplicate the account of the first; it occupies almost twice as many pages, for the narration of events is accompanied by an increasing amount of discussion of their significance. The poet has become dimly aware that there is a recurring pattern in his experiences, and it is now all the more imperative that he should discover what principle governs these events.

In order to understand the meaning of his recurrent attitudes of hopefulness and despair, the poet determines to make use of his dreams: 'L'idée me vint d'interroger le sommeil . . .' (I, 380). He has thus advanced beyond the first phase in that he is no longer dependent on the judgement or the sympathy of others, but is prepared to trust to his own intuition. He no longer hesitates before the notion that all experience is one, all consciousness continuous: he is fully convinced of the reality of his dreams, and although he can offer no rational basis for this belief ('cela est plus facile à *sentir* qu'à énoncer clairement', he remarks),[18] he is now ready—and it is a major step—to assert the validity of a mode of knowing which does not depend on reason: 'je crois que l'imagination humaine n'a rien inventé qui ne soit vrai, dans ce monde ou dans les autres'.

The dreams which begin the second phase are not at all consoling. He is disturbed by the reappearance of his Double (now dressed, like Hakem and Yousouf in the *Voyage en Orient*, 'en prince d'Orient'), and he makes a terrifying, but capital, discovery: the Double is himself. Searching for parallels to this experience, he lingers over the notion that 'L'homme est double'. The passage recalls the epigraph to *La Pandora* which Nerval took from Goethe's *Faust*: 'Deux âmes, hélas! se partagent mon sein . . .'; so that it is not surprising that he should quickly go beyond the notion of the self as both actor and spectator, to the disturbing idea of the coexistence within him of two conflicting souls, one good, one evil. The idea echoes his uncle's reminder, in the dream of the first phase, that 'La matière . . . peut se modifier selon le bien et selon le mal', and is the logical conse- quence of his having established a link between his own fortunes and those of the universe in general. But is he essentially the good or the bad soul, and will good or evil triumph? His feelings of guilt lead him to think of himself as the doomed soul; it is the mysterious Double who will triumph, and who will take the poet's place at the mystic marriage with Aurélia, as, on his first appear- ance, he had taken the poet's chance of freedom in the guard post (I, 365). But the poet cannot accept that the Double is good and himself evil, and therefore damned; in despair, he defies the 'mauvais génie' that is usurping his place: 'luttons contre l'esprit fatal, luttons contre le dieu lui-même avec les armes de la tradi- tion et de la science . . .' (I, 382). It is the mood of 'Antéros',[19] and it parallels his rejection of the apostle-figure of his friend in the first phase: 'je n'appartiens pas à ton ciel . . .' (I, 363).

Defiance does not lighten his despair: on the contrary, for it takes him further away from that 'harmonie générale' to which he aspires. Again the poet turns to his dreams for some clue to the mystery, but they remain confused. He sees again a vision of the molten centre of the earth; climbing a mountain-side, he sees a town on the further slope, and goes down 'par un escalier obscur' into its streets; here he enters a forge where artisans are working with 'le feu primitif qui anima les premiers êtres'. The passage recalls Adoniram's journey (in *Voyage en Orient*) to the heart of the mountain of Kaf, the home of his ancestors and the sanctuary of fire (II, 560). Next he finds himself in a chamber prepared for a marriage, and protests that his place is being usurped.[20] Threatened by the artisans with a red-hot rod, mocked for his impotence (the images have obvious sexual reference, as has the 'feu primitif' itself), the poet remains defiant, relying on the power of a magic sign to save him.[21] He is awakened by the cry of a woman, and feels at once that this time he has indeed gone too far: 'J'avais troublé l'harmonie de l'univers magique où mon âme puisait la certitude d'une existence immortelle'. Perhaps also he is damned for his presumption in touching the mystery, as he had been before.[22] It is clear that the way to redemption cannot lie in defiance, and that he cannot defeat the mysterious Double with a show of force, or even with 'les armes de la tradition et de la science'.

At this point, the text is divided, and the *Seconde Partie* begins. It opens with the certainty that the poet has lost Aurélia again, this time no doubt for ever. There is nothing left for him but death and damnation, for much as he desires to be engulfed in nothingness, he cannot be sure that death is indeed 'le néant'. Even God, he reflects, cannot assure him of that. He is thus led gradually to consider the idea of God's existence, and to wonder why he has for so long rejected it. It is now clear why the text is divided at this point, and not according to the two phases of his illness. The first part of *Aurélia* establishes the constant recurrence, at shorter or longer intervals, of a spiritual crisis accompanied by a sense of doom which destroys the transient certainties that the poet tries to establish for himself. The beginning of the *Seconde Partie* marks the beginning of the road to redemption, with the poet's recognition and acceptance of the central problem: his relationship to the God he had deliberately neglected.

The poet considers that his rejection of God was the result of an intellectual decision, but he does not make the mistake of asking for intellectual conviction; indeed he recognises that rational philosophy cannot help him.[23] The name of Jesus once made him weep, and it is those tears that he asks God to restore to him. In a paragraph which echoes the beginning of *Sylvie* (I, 242) he meditates on the difficulty of simple faith for a man educated in the traditions of rational thought: 'L'ignorance ne s'apprend pas', and one cannot abdicate the use of one's reason, which is itself God-given. He speaks of the authority of religion in terms of father and child: 'Dieu appréciera la pureté des intentions sans doute, et quel est le père qui se complairait à voir son fils abdiquer devant lui tout raisonnement et toute fierté!' It is clear that whether he recognises it or not, the emotional barriers between the poet and his own stern father are partly the cause of his difficulties; it is surely not accidental that his consoling dreams so constantly take him back to the childhood world in which he lived before his father came to claim him. His action in demanding from God a tribute to human reason is exactly like his defiance of the Double, whom he proposed, in the same way, to confront with 'les armes de la tradition et de la science'. He knows now, however, that this attitude will not solve his problem. Since a priest will offer him only the tenets of a single faith, he turns to esoteric books, and from them, and from his inner conviction that there must be a world of spirit outside the terrestrial world, he derives the notion that successive religions have each perceived some portion of that eternal truth which the human mind has always sought—but that none of them possesses the key to all the mysteries.[24] It is evident that, however indirectly, he is still relying on reason, and still unable to accept authority.

The account of the poet's meditations breaks off here, and he tells us how he went to visit a sick friend. With his pale face, black beard and feverish eyes, the friend has now a mystic appearance: 'il y avait en lui un apôtre' (I, 388). The incident parallels the intervention of the apostle-like friend in the first phase (I, 363); but this time the poet is willing to accept the portent: God, he realises, is with the sick man, because his friend believes that it is so:[25] but the poet himself is damned, because he defied the spirit of God, the Double whom he mistook for an enemy. His first reaction is one of despair: he has now lost Aurélia for ever. We seem to be back to the hopelessness of the first lines of the *Seconde Partie*, but the poet takes an important step forward when he realises the cause of his error: 'j'ai préféré la créature au créateur' (I, 389); because he was intent on possessing Aurélia, who seemed to him a divine mediator through whom he might be saved, he has first neglected and then challenged God himself. He must now seek repentance, for God may yet pardon him 'si je m'humilie devant lui'[26]—it is precisely what he had previously refused to do. Meeting a funeral procession, he joins the mourners on an impulse, as a 'frère de douleurs'; and in this act of charity and communion he finds a sudden release of the soul, and is able to hope and to pray.

The moment of grace, imperfect as it is, does not last. The cemetery is the one in which Aurélia is buried, and he is immediately caught up again in his obsession with her memory. He is filled with sadness, and dreams that night that Aurélia holds out her hand to him. This dream parallels the dream in the first phase in which Aurélia seemed to pardon him. But this time he is not sure of his pardon. He is awaited at a distant house, and stumbles through stones and thorns (as he did in the dream in which he pursued the goddess in the garden); he tires of the straightest path and seeks a gentler road through the woods; and thus he loses his way and arrives too late. He has lost his last chance of pardon, and lost Aurélia too. Awaking in anguish, he prays that she at least may be saved, and without quite knowing why, he destroys the relics of his love for her, including his note of the whereabouts of her grave. It is a gesture of renunciation offered to God, and it frees him at last from his obsession: Aurélia is no longer a goddess, but merely a human being like himself.

From this point, the narrative moves at an accelerated pace. There is still no easy solution in sight. Even with the central problem clear in his mind, the poet has still to live through the same recurring patterns of hopefulness, doubt and despair. Moreover his search becomes increasingly urgent in proportion to his steady acceptance of the real issues at stake, for no subterfuge can satisfy him now. His sacrifice of the relics of his earthly love leads him to hope that God will reward him with 'un sommeil moins funeste' (and here again dream is seen as a link with the universal consciousness). He recognises now that his despair has little to do with the memory of a lost love, and that the 'créature', far from being a mediator between himself and God, offered a substitute for religion that merely prevented him from establishing a direct relationship with God. Accordingly, he dreams next of a woman who had looked after him in his childhood, and whom he later failed to visit when she was dying. As in the first phase, he is attempting to replace love of one woman with love for his family,[27] past and present, which is a microcosm of the whole human race. It seems now to be too late. The old woman reproaches him with neglect of filial piety. Visions of faces he had known pass rapidly before him, falling into darkness 'comme les grains d'un chapelet dont le lien s'est brisé' (I, 392): it is the 'chaîne non interrompue' (I, 368) of which he had dreamed in the first phase, shattered now through his failure to do his share in maintaining the universal harmony. Images of antiquity suggest to him confusedly that he has failed to understand what he has learned from books, as he failed to understand the lessons of experience. Ten years after his first premonitions of death, he is again convinced that his final hour has come.

This dream has further narrowed the field in which salvation may be found: he has failed to find it not only in the love of woman, but also in the redemption offered by all the various doctrines devised by man. Yet even now, faced with the certainty of death, and miserably aware that he has wasted his life, he cannot bring himself to confess to a priest, though he is conscious of a strong urge to do so. Looking back at his past life, he tries for the first time to consider dispassionately why he is unable to turn to the church for help. The conflict implied in his previous, highly emotional discussion of this problem (at the beginning of the *Seconde Partie*) is now brought to the surface. The poet notes his inheritance of eighteenth-century 'philosophie'; without this, and his study of comparative religion (now seen clearly as an obstacle to faith), he would be able to follow his natural inclination: 'Je frémis en songeant quel chrétien je ferais . . .' (I, 393). Abruptly he remarks that he never knew his mother, while his father had no influence on his earliest notions. His contact in infancy with the myths and divinities of antiquity, his uncle's teaching that 'Dieu, c'est le soleil', and some instruction in 'les beautés et les grandeurs du christianisme',[28] understandably left the boy with 'une certaine irrésolution'. The man, even though he is now able to understand the causes of his difficulties, has still a long and unhappy path to tread before his release.

The affirmation of his guilt which he sees in his dreams reduces the poet to despair. His description of his state of mind tallies closely with classical accounts of acute depression, and repeats the description of the crisis of 1841 which we find in a letter to his father written in 1842 (I, 909). The first lightening of his despair is again mediated by a friend, who like his previous consolers seems to have a religious aura, 'presque cénobitique' (I, 395), and in whose words Nerval believes he hears the voice of Providence. Encouraged by fortuitous signs, as before, he determines by way of repentance to repair all the evil he may have done in his life, beginning with an apology for a minor negligence.

But his good resolution brings him a short-lived joy. Hampered by a series of inexplicable difficulties and disasters, he is unable to work and cannot fulfil his contracts. He feels incapable of repairing what now seems an enormous weight of guilt. Dogged by failure, he is overcome by consternation when his father refuses his offer to help with logs for the fire (I, 396): an apparently minor incident, but charged with all the tragedy of the poet's unrequited but constant love for his father. The crisis is such that the final inhibition is removed: seeing a priest in the street, the poet is suddenly moved to ask for confession. But the priest is on his way to an evening party and tells the poet to come tomorrow. Feeling rejected, he tries to pray in a nearby church, but it seems to him that the Virgin is dead and cannot hear him. In a second gesture of renunciation, he removes from his finger a ring inscribed with the name of Allah; but even this abnegation of his faith in other religions does not help him to pray. He thinks of suicide, and through a night of hallucination in which, like his Christ in 'Le Christ aux Oliviers', he sees 'un soleil noir dans le ciel désert' and believes that the globe is spinning at random in space,[29] he hourly expects the end of the world, convinced that Christ too is dead. His visions have now taken from him the Virgin and Christ, the two gentle mediators between God and man, leaving him with no alternative but to face God Himself at last. The next day, he turns again to a friend,[30] and is taken to a clinic.

After a month of fluctuating moods, the poet is released, and
during the brief interval before his next internment he writes 'une
de mes meilleures nouvelles': *Sylvie*. With absolute frankness, he
admits that this achievement was difficult and anguished, and
that he failed to find his balance. But in the midst of his fears and
hallucinations, he is moved to pity for a man whom he has
frightened by his eccentric behaviour, and as in the incident of
the funeral at which he wept, this renewed ability to feel for
others enables him to hope again. He goes to pray in a church,
thinks of his mother and is moved to tears. His despair begins to
lift, and he goes at once to visit his father again. Finding that his
father is not at home, he leaves flowers for him (his choice is a
bunch of marguerites, and though he does not refer to the fact,
we know that Marguerite was his mother's name). He wanders
the streets seeing signs of hope everywhere. Exhausted, he falls
asleep in a friend's house and dreams that the goddess Isis
appears to him with the promise of final salvation. As always,
growing elation leads to irrational feelings of guilt, and his
behaviour becomes increasingly eccentric, leading to his return
to the clinic, where he is put into a strait-jacket. Escaping, he
tries to cure some of the patients by laying on of hands; believing
that he has god-like powers of healing (and thinking perhaps of
his father, who was a doctor), he rejects the idea that man may
be healed by science alone (I, 400–1). This rejection of science
might appear to be a tacit admission of the impotence of 'les
armes de la tradition et de la science' with which he had once
defied the Double and 'le dieu lui-même' (I, 382). But Nerval
still seems to be trying to equate himself with the deity, since he
claims that he possesses supernatural powers. His desire to seek
redemption by humbling himself before God seems now to have
been forgotten. He is soon recaptured, put back into the strait-
jacket, and taken to another clinic outside Paris; here, seeing
himself among the mentally ill, he realises that he has been
suffering from delusions. Yet he is convinced of the reality of his
vision of the goddess Isis, and believes that all these sufferings
are meant to test him, that he is undergoing the trials of an
initiation. The goddess, it is clear, has again been interposed
between himself and God, and since she is both 'la mère et
l'épouse sacrée', and 'la même que ta mère' (I, 404, 399), he now

has himself the status of a god: 'j'étais devenu semblable à un dieu' (I, 400).

The notion of an initiation allows the poet to see a purpose in what is happening to him. A vision of his family as an endless procession on horseback leads him, as in the dream of his uncle's house in the first phase, to a sudden apprehension of a universal family. This time the unity embraces the natural world, and in a passage of great lyrical beauty, Nerval celebrates the sense of communion which the vision brings him.[31] But his joy is almost immediately disturbed by the realisation of what must logically follow: if he is eternally bound to the world of Creation, he is at the mercy of whatever spirit rules that order—and as his uncle had warned him, it might well fall into the power of a spirit of evil. He is disturbed by the thought that the goddess Isis, like the Virgin of whom she is an avatar, may no longer be able to help him.

Caught as always between alternating hope and despair, the poet is finally rescued by his doctor's intelligent attempts to interest him in the fate of a fellow-patient. Once more charity proves stronger than melancholy, and the poet is released from the 'cercle monotone' of obsession with his own griefs, by the sympathy and pity he feels for the young man (I, 407). In a radiant dream, he hears the young man call him 'frère', and the goddess Isis tells him that this is the mediator his salvation required, 'une âme simple et dégagée des liens de la terre' (I, 408). A simple faith, it will be remembered, was what he knew to be necessary, but exceedingly difficult to achieve.

The text of *Aurélia* continues with a series of dreams under the title *Mémorables*.[32] The experiences recounted up to this point have shown an equal proportion of consoling and terrifying visions, filling the poet alternately with hope and despair. In the *Mémorables*, though not everything seems intelligible to the dreamer, it is clear at least that the mood is steadily hopeful, and even joyful. The first section in particular (I, 409–11; the Pléiade edition prints a line of dots at the beginning and end of this section), is lyrical and exalted, a hymn of joy and thanksgiving in which the certainty of pardon and salvation is unclouded by doubts either about God's goodness or about the poet's own fitness. Most significant of all, in this section the poet finally achieves the most difficult of all reconciliations: that with the father-god, who appears here in the guise of Thor, the god of thunder (I, 411): 'le pardon du Christ a été aussi prononcé pour toi! Sois donc béni toi-même, ô Thor, le géant . . .'[33]

At the end of *Mémorables*, the poet returns to an account of his efforts to analyse his experiences, and in particular, of his resolve to 'fixer le rêve' and learn its secrets. This passage repeats in essence the introduction to the account of the first phase of the poet's illness,[34] except that it seems less hesitant, more ready to make the effort of will required to force an understanding from the mysteries of existence: 'dominer mes sensations au lieu de les subir'. There is no trace here, however, of Romantic revolt or spiritual presumption; it is rather a question of having the courage to accept responsibility for oneself, to remain unhampered by excessive guilt, and like Prometheus to reach through love, extended even to those who do not offer love in return,[35] a perfect reconciliation. The poet is thus enabled to emerge from despair and 'rentrer dans les voies lumineuses de la religion'.

Nerval's doctor, Emile Blanche, was a compassionate and unusually intelligent man, as Nerval recognised,[36] and he encouraged the poet to 'write out' his conflicts in the hope that he would thereby be released from them. By applying his natural gifts of analytical intelligence to his own experiences, Nerval does seem to have arrived at an understanding of his problems from within, where previously he had looked outside himself, in literature and in life, for models which could help him to understand his divided self. It is possible to see the act of writing *Aurélia* as an epitome of the very struggles it records and seeks to analyse. If Nerval set out, as I have suggested, to produce a justification of his life, and not only an explanation of it, the desire for justification may be seen as itself a symptom of his inability to reconcile himself with God. It is a measure of the poet's good faith that when he became aware of this fact, he continued to look steadily into his mind and to record, as dispassionately as he could, what he saw there. Yet another trap awaited him: merely to attempt to explain supposes a belief in the efficacy of human reason, which is, as we have seen, one of the chief obstacles to simple faith. Of this also he became aware, and with characteristic lucidity learned to take it into account.

There is finally a victory for the poet in *Aurélia*, and one which he achieves nowhere else. Perhaps not unexpectedly, he achieves it at the point where analytical reasoning gives way to lyrical feeling, when the inhibitions of self-protection are swept away by a child-like trust in ultimate goodness, so that the poet is able to extend his love to the whole of creation. This consummation is celebrated in the *Mémorables* in a splendid stream of poetic images. But there is no attempt at the discipline of poetic *form*, and it is not the least part of Nerval's tragedy that he did not live to write the poems which might have given to this intense experience the kind of ordered finality which he achieves elsewhere. We have to recognise, however, that the values which concern Nerval in *Aurélia* are essentially more human than literary. It is a uniquely honest account of a painful spiritual progress, and as Nerval himself remarked in *Promenades et Souvenirs* (I, 133): 'l'expérience de chacun est le trésor de tous'.

NERVAL'S REPUTATION AND INFLUENCE

Nerval's life and work have been obscured by legend both during his lifetime and since his death, though the particular form of the legend has undergone some curious reversals. Mirecourt, whose biography of Nerval appeared in 1854, already shows signs of being concerned more with the myth of the poet's life than with his work.[1] Nerval's own judgement of the book is astute: 'on m'y traite en héros de roman et c'est plein d'exagérations bienveillantes sans doute et d'inexactitudes qui m'importent fort peu du reste, puisqu'il s'agit d'un personnage conventionnel . . .'[2] This 'personnage conventionnel', with the passage of time, was repeatedly modified as conventions changed.

A useful corrective to Mirecourt's view appears in Baudelaire's article on Hégésippe Moreau (1861), in which he compares Nerval with Edgar Allan Poe.[3] Poe he thought the greater genius; but he esteems them both above all as 'd'excellents hommes de lettres, . . . travaillant, il est vrai, à leurs heures, à leur guise, selon une méthode plus ou moins mystérieuse, mais actifs, industrieux, utilisant leurs rêveries ou leurs méditations; bref, exerçant allégrement leur profession'. Another contemporary view, from the opposite side of the Channel, was not so enchanted as Baudelaire with Nerval's professionalism. An unsigned article entitled 'A Trio of French Tourists' (*Blackwood's Magazine*, March 1853) discussed travel books by Gautier, Méry and Nerval. *Blackwood's* did not in general approve of French travel books, suspecting them to be the work of professional writers 'who set off with the deliberate intention of making their journey pay itself'. Nerval survives the English scrutiny rather better than Gautier or Méry; but while praising in Nerval's *Lorely* 'the playful style in which he excels', the English critic found it at the most 'an example of a trite subject happily handled'. This attitude is reflected in our own time by Peter Quennell, who deplores 'Gérard's professionalism, his mechanical aptitude for writing . . .', a fault hardly redeemed by the 'dozen poems that ballast his reputation'.[4] Among his contemporaries, however, Nerval was respected as an honest and honourable member of his profession. Heinrich Heine, like Baudelaire, recognised that Nerval's apparent spontaneity went hand in hand with patient craftsmanship: 'La diction de Gérard coulait avec une pureté suave, qui était inimitable, et qui ne ressemblait qu'à l'incomparable douceur de son âme ... Et c'était un grand artiste; les parfums de sa pensée étaient toujours enfermés dans des cassolettes d'or merveilleusement ciselées'.[5] Arsène Houssaye likewise regarded Nerval as 'un poète de la grande école', and praised his artistic judgement.[6]

Théophile Gautier saw Nerval as a writer in the classical tradition, something of an exception in his turbulent times: 'Gérard était parmi nous le seul lettré dans l'acception où se prenait ce mot au milieu du 18ème siècle'. He particularly praises the quality of Nerval's language, echoing Heine's appreciation of its 'pureté': 'peu de littérateurs de notre temps ont une langue plus châtiée, plus nette et plus transparente ... le style du 18ème siècle lui suffit ... il s'abstint toujours des violentes colorations dont nous avons tous plus ou moins abusé ... le seul défaut qu'on puisse peut-être lui reprocher, c'est trop de sagesse'. An article published when Nerval died also commended his exceptional restraint, 'sa tenue si parfaite de dignité et de modestie à une époque où l'art de se vanter soi-même est devenu si impudent'.[7] Gautier was aware that certain of his friend's last writings were scarcely likely to be accused of 'trop de sagesse'; but he insisted that Nerval never lost artistic control of his work: 'jamais son sens littéraire ne fut altéré'. 'L'étrangeté la plus inouïe se revêt, chez Gérard de Nerval, de formes pour ainsi dire classiques', he remarked. He does not discuss this 'strangeness', but merely refers briefly in his *Notice* of 1854 to 'certaines allures d'illuminé', adding that this tendency was more than counter-balanced by the 'réalité parfaite' of the studies in *Les Illuminés* and by the limpid clarity of *Sylvie*.[8]

For the rest, Nerval's contemporaries tended to repeat with more or less affectionate amusement the current anecdotes recounting (and frequently inventing) his eccentricities. These legends, retailed at length in Arsène Houssaye's *Confessions* and in Champfleury's *Grandes Figures*,[9] have proved remarkably durable. Nerval's periodic madness was undoubtedly a barrier to understanding, even with his closest friends. What appeared inconsequent or obscure in his work was too easily attributed to mental disorder. Nerval, for his part, talked about himself as little as possible, and it was not until the last year of his life that he attempted, encouraged by his doctor, to write a reasoned account of his experiences. But *Aurélia* is not very easy of access, and many of its first readers must have dismissed it at once as the eloquent ravings of a charming lunatic. In general Nerval's contemporaries tended to see a division in his work between the sane and the insane, the reasonable and the unreasonable. This artificial division has endured until recent years; it proved to have a two-fold effect: on the one hand, the 'difficult' works, severed from the main body of his writings, acquired a false autonomy which permitted the wildest of interpretations; on the other, their exclusion meant that any account of their author was necessarily incomplete, and often deliberately so.

After the poet's death, his reputation became obscured in France—though oddly enough not in England, where Andrew Lang wrote of Nerval in 1871.[10] His account of Nerval as a 'modern scholar-gipsy' infected by what Matthew Arnold called the 'strange disease of modern life', is occasionally acute but more often marred by romanticising ('that light and tameless soul from the dreamed-of ways and waters of the Hollow Land'). So intent is Lang on painting a 'Bohemian' portrait that he is led to remark that for Nerval 'a home (was) a mere piece of pedantry': a good example of the way in which legend can blind Nerval's critics to the most patent truths. George Saintsbury attempts a more scholarly appraisal in 1880, finding Nerval 'but little if at all less distinguished' than Gautier in poetry, prose, literary and art criticism, and travel writings.[11] In 1882 he remarked that Nerval's prose often approaches the nature of 'prose poetry', while his verse 'lies on the further side between poetry and music'.[12] Finally, in his *History of the French Novel*, Saintsbury rescues Nerval from the category of 'minors', and finds in him 'a strange and exquisite charm' which he thinks is commoner in England or in the Germany of Nerval's own time than it is in France, 'and, in Gérard's peculiar brand of it, almost entirely unknown'.[13]

In France, in the memoirs of those who had known him, Nerval was remembered for his personality rather than for his work. However, in February 1887 the *Revue Wagnérienne* reprinted Nerval's articles on Wagner (originally published in *La Presse* in 1850 and incorporated into *Lorely* in 1852). The part he played in introducing Wagner's music in France was shortly afterwards acknowledged by Georges Servières;[14] and in this highly accidental fashion Nerval the poet was brought to the notice of the Symbolists.[15]

The Symbolists, as one might expect, chose the 'difficult' aspects of Nerval for their special consideration; but their view of the poet inclines essentially towards Mirecourt's rather than towards Baudelaire's description. Gustave Kahn,[16] for instance, has little time for Nerval's prose writings, and none for his plays or journalism; he is mostly concerned with 'ce grand développement du rêve, ou mieux, cette ascension vers l'âme qui émane de ses grandes œuvres et de ses vers définitifs'—that is, *Les Chimères*. Kahn discourses at considerable length on the subject of love, and in his description Nerval becomes a 'modern lover' of the kind which the late nineteenth century understood: 'Cet amour aigu, douloureux, mysticisme de l'amour, léthargie de l'acte, hyperesthésie de l'âme, maladie plutôt qu'amour, plus que tout autre Gérard de Nerval en gravit le chemin de croix'. Nerval's realism and humour, which his contemporaries much appreciated, would evidently be quite out of place in this particular universe. His wanderings, his amiable and innocent fascination with the world around him, seem to Kahn, as his industry seemed to Mirecourt, wholly a necessary distraction, 'qui le dérobait aux intimes et bourrelles préoccupations'. Kahn presents Nerval as a conscious stranger to the frivolous world of his contemporaries, 'très sûr de sa supériorité d'érudition, d'élégance et de vraie force poétique sur ceux de son âge, mais assez dédaigneux de se répandre en parades . . .' Even were it true to life, this dæmonic figure (which seems to owe a good deal to Baudelaire's *dandy*) would be at best a very limited portrait of Nerval.

In 1897 there appeared a slim, elegant little book entitled *Les Chimères et Les Cydalises*, with a preface by Rémy de Gourmont in which he formally claimed Nerval as a forerunner of the Symbolist movement, 'frère de Baudelaire, de Verlaine et de Mallarmé'.[17] Henri de Régnier, reviewing this edition,[18] praises the sonnets for 'leur chant sybillin . . . leurs pierreries châtoyantes', and accepts

Nerval as the Symbolists' spiritual ancestor: 'Leur contagieuse beauté hanta des rêves fraternels. Je croirais bien que M. Stéphane Mallarmé l'a ressentie profondément. Baudelaire en connut le frisson jumeau . . .' These judgements clearly influenced Arthur Symons, ambassador extraordinary in England for the French literature of his time, who in the following year wrote at considerable length about Nerval. Symons is responsible for the renewed interest in Nerval's work in England in the early thirties, for by describing him as a pre-Symbolist he ensured Nerval's acceptance by the Imagist poets, who would certainly have rejected him if they had thought he was a Romantic. It was from Symons, too, that T. S. Eliot learned of Nerval, and a line from 'El Desdichado' found its way into *The Waste Land* (1922). Symons, in company with the Symbolists, dismisses a large part of Nerval's work, and would retain only 'the sonnets, *Le Rêve et la Vie*, and *Sylvie*; of which *Sylvie* is the most objectively achieved, a wandering idyl . . .; *Le Rêve et la Vie* being the most intensely personal, a narrative of madness, unique as madness itself; and the sonnets, a kind of miracle, which may be held to have created something at least of the method of the later Symbolists'. Symons claims that Nerval was the first to use in French 'words which create an atmosphere by the actual suggestive quality of their syllables, as, according to the theory of Mallarmé, they should do . . .' However, Symons is inclined to doubt whether Nerval was aware of this.[19] Here again, while Symons makes the highest claims for *Les Chimères*, Nerval is a shadowy figure, and even that shadow, one feels, is borrowed from Gustave Kahn: 'It was with disdain, as well as with confidence, that he allowed these sonnets to be overheard'.[20] 'Le bon Gérard' seems to have vanished utterly, to be replaced by another conventional figure, a 'poète maudit' of the kind described by Verlaine in 1884.

How well did the Symbolists understand the poems they rated so highly? In his introduction to *Les Filles du Feu* (I, 158–9), Nerval remarked of his own sonnets that 'Ils ne sont guère plus obscurs que la métaphysique d'Hégel ou les *Mémorables* de Swedenborg, et perdraient de leur charme à être expliqués, si la chose était possible; concédez-moi du moins le mérite de l'expression'. It is fairly certain that in this passage Nerval was mocking his friend Dumas.[21] But Henri de Régnier welcomed what he mistook for Nerval's indifference to the meaning of his poems, and he praises above all the beauty of their sound: 'ces vers, avec quelque chose de suprême et d'inachevé en leur sens comme en leur forme, s'apparentent à ce que la poésie a de plus secret et de plus beau et l'on désire moins scruter leur énigme qu'obéir au charme inexplicable de leur harmonieuse incantation'. It would seem that the relative inaccessibility of Nerval's mature works, which had hindered their acceptance among his contemporaries, was a positive recommendation in the eyes of the Symbolist critics: Régnier's juxtaposition of *suprême* and *inachevé* suggests that a premium is being placed on mystery.

Any influence or value attributed to Nerval at this time was felt to derive above all from *Aurélia* and from *Les Chimères*. Nerval himself claimed to have written his sonnets in an 'état de rêverie super-naturaliste' (I, 158). This term is open to a variety of interpretations, and only by tracing it to its source in Heine can one appreciate what Nerval meant it to signify; but it was no doubt this term which was the signal for his adoption by the Surrealists, who equated 'super-naturaliste' with 'surréaliste'.[22] Arguing then from effect to cause, we reach a position in which Nerval is seen as the precursor of later schools of poetry. In our own day S. A. Rhodes emphatically endorses these claims: 'Gérard de Nerval may well be credited, as well as Baudelaire, with the spiritual paternity of symbolist and post-symbolist poetry'.[23] Later poets have indeed frequently felt some kinship with Nerval; but it does not in the least follow that they shared the same temperament or experience, or even the same motives. Nerval's term 'super-naturaliste' is not to be equated unreservedly with Surrealism. Nerval would never have glorified the defeat of the conscious mind and of the human will, as the Surrealists did. All his efforts were directed towards maintaining full control of his mental world: 'diriger mon rêve éternel au lieu de le subir' ('Paradoxe et Vérité'; I, 429). In her study of Surrealism, Anna Balakian explicitly rejects Nerval as a source of Surrealist art, emphasising his rational objectives and his efforts to control and harmonise his visions and his beliefs; while in Surrealism she finds 'a mysticism that denies harmony in art and life'.[24] Moreover, Nerval's fusion of reason and dream has a moral objective, and in this he differs also from the Symbolists, for whom, Béguin has said, dream was a source of imagery and 'un précieux modèle proposé à leurs recherches esthétiques . . .'[25] Aesthetic considerations are of secondary importance to Nerval. In certain respects, then, the Symbolists' and the Surrealists' adoption of Nerval was the result of a fundamental misapprehension.[26]

Meanwhile, however high he stood in the estimation of the active literary minorities at the end of the nineteenth and in the early twentieth century, Nerval had still not received recognition from the leaders of academic criticism (indeed, he has always been more quickly appreciated by his fellow writers, and especially by poets, than by critics). His first 'notice' of this kind was written by Emile Faguet in 1906, in a review of the newly-published biography of Nerval by Gauthier-Ferrières.[27] Faguet's first concern was to 'place' Nerval in the history of French literature (though the histories of French literature did not accord him even a mention until much later):

Il avait sa note à lui, très rapprochée, à la vérité, de celle de Théophile Gautier, mais bien à lui cependant, d'un romantisme plus allemand, je veux dire plus intime, plus pénétré, plus pénétrant, plus sourd aussi, je le reconnais, tout compte fait très particulier, et qui fait de Gérard, selon moi, un intermédiaire assez exact entre Théophile Gautier et Baudelaire.

Faguet has obviously chosen the course of ignoring the 'difficult' works. He praises the poem 'Fantaisie', which he likens to 'Gautier première manière', and admires 'Avril' from the *Odelettes*, which reminds him of Théophile de Viaud. He makes no mention of *Aurélia* or of *Les Filles du Feu*. Of *Les Chimères*, only 'Delfica' is considered; this poem, he says, 'nous entraîne avec des mots précis et des images nettes vers un passé confus, indéterminé, indéfini et inquiétant'; the observation is both penetrating and pertinent, the inevitable comparison—with Nietzsche's *Zarathustra*!—rather less so. Faguet reproaches Gauthier-Ferrières with devoting too much space to the poet's life at the expense of his work. Nevertheless he also feels bound to comment on Nerval's life, and in particular on his madness: 'La folie de Gérard a été, à mon très humble jugement et très peu informé, assez complexe. Il me semble qu'elle était composée de manie itinérante et de quelque folie des grandeurs'. This view constituted for many years what one may call the 'official' estimate of Nerval. Only those works are praised which can be shown to have an affinity with the work of other, already accepted writers; what is strange or difficult tends to be neglected; and the poet himself, his madness neatly 'defined' according to one or more accepted diagnostic labels, is relegated to a decent obscurity.

When Aristide Marie published his justly celebrated biography of Nerval in 1914, the wheel came full circle. Marie, unmoved by the claims of the Symbolists, like Gautier praised 'le classique, pénétré de claire tradition, qu'il n'a cessé d'être', emphasising Nerval's grace, irony and lucidity.[28] The inevitable result was that *Sylvie* and the *Odelettes* came to be prized as the summit of his achievement, while *Aurélia* and *Les Chimères* were correspondingly underrated. They might be allowed a certain strange beauty, but it was felt that they were basically the work of an unbalanced mind, while *La Pandora* was decidedly incoherent. This view of course accords well with Faguet's appraisal, with this difference: that far from being 'très peu informé', Aristide Marie had steeped himself in his subject. Such unconscious evasions as one finds in Marie's work are attributable, without a doubt, to his affection for his poet.

Aristide Marie's judgement of *Les Chimères*,[29] which seems like Faguet to refer to Nietzschean ideals, initiates an important trend in twentieth-century criticism of Nerval:

Il est maintenant tout à l'extase dont l'ont ravi les demi-dieux de l'hellénisme, les Orphée et les Pythagore; il voudrait réveiller les échos de leur chant divin, cette alliance de la Poésie et de la Musique, qui, sur la lyre d'ivoire ou la cithare d'or, a révélé le secret de l'harmonie des mondes, dans la pure lumière de Dionysos . . .

It is implied that the objectives of *Les Chimères* were a new departure for Nerval; that these poems embody 'une vague aspiration', foredoomed to failure, towards a mystical and ultimate consummation. This view of Nerval's later work has been widespread, with variations only in the emphasis, some critics insisting rather on the strength of the mystical urge, and others on the pathos of the failure. In either case, there was a point in the poet's life beyond which his work was no longer judged as literature, but only as a reflection of the tragedy of his fate. From this point it is but a step to the romanticising kind of biographical study. Thus the portraits drawn by Francis Carco, by René Bizet, or by Henri Clouard[30] are more concerned with the drama of the poet's life than with his work.

Though the centenary of the Romantic Revolution, officially celebrated in France in 1927, led to more widespread interest in many 'minor' Romantics, including Nerval, his place in the history of French literature, so neatly pin-pointed by Faguet as 'un intermédiaire assez exact entre Théophile Gautier et Baudelaire', was not greatly challenged or altered. Nor is it in more recent accounts, except that new links have been added to Faguet's chain. Alice Coléno,[31] for instance, begins the line with Nerval and follows it through Baudelaire to Rimbaud and Mallarmé, finding in all four poets the same aspirations and the same frustrations, the same inevitable failure to reach the same exalted vision. René Lalou, however, makes an important distinction between Nerval and Baudelaire: 'tandis que pour Baudelaire la pureté sera la suprême conquête de l'artiste, elle est chez Nerval l'état naturel de son imagination'.[32] Edmund Wilson also speaks of Baudelaire's 'passion for literature which has managed to burn pure and intense through suffering and degradation';[33] this artistic purity, which Wilson suggests has nothing to do with religion, seems to me to be a very different ideal from Nerval's, which was rather a spiritual purity, a fitness to enter the Kingdom of Heaven as he conceived it. I am even less inclined to liken Nerval to Rimbaud and to Mallarmé. These poets—in their quite different ways—pitted themselves against the universe, seeing poetry as an instrument of magical supremacy. Nerval's prayer that he might be allowed to 'diriger mon rêve éternel au lieu de le subir' is firstly a plea for participation, a wish to take an active part in the creation of a universe of harmony; and it is secondly a plea for survival, for Nerval never willingly yielded to that desire for self-annihilation which lies at the bottom of so much later poetry, the horrified fascination with 'le néant', whether insanity or death. He did not seek escape; and indeed his failure to reach the star he followed, which Alice Coléno compares with Rimbaud's 'Echec', and Mallarmé's defeat,[34] was not in fact to him a tragedy at all: he was recalled by 'le regret de la terre et de ceux que j'y aimais' (I, 364), and seems to have been half glad of it.

When literary criticism began to make use of the terminology and ideas of the psychologists, Nerval was once more reconsidered in the light of current theory. It has even been suggested that psychology has saved Nerval from oblivion: 'A lowly niche in literary history as a forerunner of the Symbolist school would have seemed a fair assumption regarding Nerval twenty years ago. But modern interest in psychology has found a new significance in his work . . . His dreams are the ingenuous outpourings of his unconscious'.[35] So writes A. J. Leventhal in 1941, and proceeds to discuss Nerval entirely as an interesting case of schizophrenia. He was, I believe, no such thing; but even if the psychology were more profound, one would still question the value of the approach. Would Nerval not have preferred the 'lowly niche', where at least he retained the dignity of the artist?[36] The new approach was little concerned with art. Its business was to demonstrate in the artist certain clearly-labelled 'complexes', a process not dissimilar to definition by 'influences' and 'schools' in the field of literature; and the end result is commonly yet another 'personnage conventionnel'. Just as an 'Oedipus complex' or a father-fixation do not and cannot *explain* a Hamlet (in the sense of explaining him away), a study of Nerval such as that made by L.-H. Sebillotte,[37] while it makes explicit certain half-divined themes in the work of Nerval, is incomplete in that it excludes the characteristic diversity of Nerval's achievement and interests, and misleading in so far as it claims to have 'explained everything'. A predictable result of the new interest in 'psycho-analytical' criticism, in Nerval's case, was that the image of him as a 'classical' writer was obscured, and he came to be seen again as 'le ténébreux', the poet of mystery, of *Aurélia* and *Les Chimères*. The mystery, however, was no longer enjoyed for its own sake: it challenged the critic to explain it.

Nerval is no longer neglected and underrated. In 1947 Michaud, in his study of Symbolist poetry,[38] named Nerval and Poe as the two prime movers in 'le passage du Romantique au moderne'. Béguin also sees Nerval as the first of the moderns: 'Les premières années du Second Empire virent naître . . . les trois œuvres capitales qui sont à la source de toute la poésie

moderne: l'*Aurélia* de Nerval avec les *Chimères* qui en sont insépa-
rables, les *Fleurs du Mal*, et enfin les poèmes mythiques de Hugo'.[39]
Behind these judgements lie some familiar assumptions. Michaud,
for instance, while leaving Nerval in much the same place as
that to which Faguet assigned him ('un intermédiaire assez exact
entre Théophile Gautier et Baudelaire'), sees him as a great
innovator: the point is made by linking him with Edgar Allan
Poe; but like Kahn, he tends to assimilate Nerval to his own
conception of what art—and therefore the artist—should be, and
offers us a very limited view of Nerval's work. Béguin likewise
attributes Nerval's importance only to *Aurélia* and *Les Chimères*.
In the context, the claim is justified, but again, it presents us
with a view of Nerval which is incomplete, and in some respects
misleading. Y.-G. Le Dantec in the introduction to his edition of *Les
Chimères*, where the sonnets, beautifully printed, stand in splendid
and significant isolation, takes this process to its logical end:[40]

Il reste que *Les Chimères*, ne fût-ce qu'en vertu de leurs prodigieuses
résonnances et des échos que leur musique miraculeuse a propagés,
dominent de très haut, et définitivement, après une longue période de
demi-indifférence ou de légèreté, un siècle tout entier de notre histoire
et de notre évolution poétiques. Miracle d'autant plus bouleversant que
l'on conçoit avec peine comment ces alexandrins d'une musculature
vraiment divine aient jailli du même cerveau que plusieurs milliers de
petits vers faciles ou fades . . .

But the man who wrote the 'petits vers' (as well as a great deal
of prose) and the man who wrote *Les Chimères*, are indeed one
and the same; by isolating the sonnets, we literally deprive them
of their context, leaving a 'musique' so disembodied as to allow
of the most subjective interpretations.

Fundamentally, modern criticism of Nerval maintains the
artificial divisions we have observed in his nineteenth-century
critics' accounts of him, although in general we tend to value
most what his contemporaries preferred to set aside, and dismiss
what they praised; so that most current valuations of his work
concur roughly with that of the Symbolists, though often for
different reasons.

In 1955 the centenary of Nerval's death, marked by an exhibition at the Bibliothèque nationale in Paris, intensified and
extended interest in the poet. Much patient and scholarly effort

has gone into the examination of Nerval's sources, and into detailed *explication de texte*. Recent attempts at interpretation reflect the divergent trends of modern critical methods. Many of these methods, unfortunately, in spite of their coherence as theoretical systems, are applicable only to rather narrowly defined aspects of individual writers. An admittedly extreme example is the astrological approach of Jean Richer, who finds that the basis of Nerval's poetic art is numerological, and the course of his existence pre-determined by his horoscope, of which he was aware.[41] Whether one believes in astrology and arithmosophy or not, it is clear that their exclusive application to the interpretation of Nerval's work produces a curiously one-sided view of his activity; and the same is true of Freudian, Jungian, alchemical-esoteric, verbal-associational or structuralist analysis of the texts: each of these disciplines may have something to contribute to the understanding of a complex body of work, but none alone can claim to define what is specifically character-istic of Nerval—indeed, they frequently succeed only in empha-sising those elements of his art which are common to all literature belonging to the European tradition—to say nothing of those which are simply human. We certainly cannot ignore the fact that Nerval's boundless curiosity and his search for parallels to his own experience led him into many unexpected paths. It seems to the present writer however that whatever he chose to incor-porate into his work, whether it came from history or mythology, from alchemy or the Tarot, from the plastic arts, from literature or from his own experience, was altered by his choice of it: whatever may be the significance of these things in other contexts, in the context of Nerval's work they acquire a meaning which is wholly Nervalian.

Finally, there is the reaction from exegesis, typified by Béguin as early as 1936; he says of Nerval's sonnets: 'De patientes recherches ont pu en retrouver les éléments dans la biographie ou dans les lectures du poète; mais toutes les tentatives d'intrusion logique sont restées vaines, car nul ne peut savoir exactement ce qui rendait chacun de ces éléments irremplaçable . . .' Twenty long years and much exegesis later, Aunos also concludes: 'Les Chimères semblent sortir d'un monde onirique. Leurs significa-tions sont si multiples que l'on peut employer toutes les clefs imaginables pour pénétrer leur secret sans qu'elles cessent jamais de nous paraître inabordables'.[42] Thus the tendency of the Symbolists to emphasise the mysterious music of *Les Chimères* and to set aside their meaning, is a solution still in favour. In 1926, Henri Bremond cited *Les Chimères* as an example of poetry which can be recited 'avec ferveur' while its meaning remains totally obscure.[43] Y.-G. Le Dantec is fundamentally in agreement:[44]

Pour mon humble part, je ne me permettrai pas de conclure dans le sens d'un hermétisme susceptible d'explication ni dans celui d'une splendeur gratuite ou simplement incohérente. Que nous parvenions ou non un jour à découvrir toutes les 'clefs' de cette incomparable séquence, la jouissance auditive et intellectuelle que nous en tirons s'en trouvera-t-elle accrue? J'en doute fort . . .

G. Rouger likewise doubts the possibility—and even the wisdom —of understanding the sonnets, and concludes: 'Qu'il nous suffise—et nous y trouverons plus sûrement notre joie—d'écouter les vers des *Chimères* "avec délices, comme de la musique" '.[45] There is a danger here of lapsing into the kind of passive 'appreciation' in which the reader is chiefly aware of his own responses. André Lebois, whose examination of *Les Chimères* is less capricious than many recent studies of Nerval, insists on the futility of regarding these sonnets as so much disembodied sound:[46]

Les Chimères ne sont pas poésie *pure*, si la locution devait impliquer réussite verbale au détriment de la pensée; elles contiennent tout le drame, intellectuel, moral, sentimental, de l'être le plus tourmenté qui fut jamais. Notre admiration n'est pas diminuée par la connaissance de ce drame: au contraire!

In truth, this drama is contained not merely in *Les Chimères*, but in all Nerval's work. The problem is to steer a reasonable course between too much preoccupation with 'l'être le plus tourmenté qui fut jamais' and too radical a separation of the work from the man who, in writing, had certain intentions, aims and preoccupations which we ignore at our peril. In a sensitive and eminently sensible article, Alison Fairlie recommends that we interrogate the text itself, as 'something that should make its central effect unaided'.[47] Her own conclusion is that the core of what Nerval is trying to convey is 'the shift of mood from chaos to pattern, from terror to consolation . . .' I have tried to suggest answers to the questions which remain: what caused the shifts of mood; what kind of pattern he envisaged, and why; how far he was instrumental in creating, as distinct from passively experiencing, that pattern; in what spirit he wished to 'convey' it to others. We are certainly most likely to find the answers to these questions in the text itself—if by 'the text' we understand not only the poem or story which we have before us at a given moment, but the whole body of Nerval's work.

Though recent criticism of Nerval shows a renewed interest in some of his minor writings, it is generally in an attempt to throw light on the major works which continue to engage most of the critical attention devoted to Nerval: 'El Desdichado', *Sylvie*, *Voyage en Orient* and particularly *Aurélia*; James Villas, in 1967, refers to *Aurélia* as 'the work considered by most scholars to be Gérard's masterpiece'.[48] The 'return to the text' which Alison Fairlie recommended in 1961 and of which Raymond Jean saw welcome signs in 1959,[49] has helped to dispel some of the most persistent elements of the legend whose development we have sketched here, and in particular to show that, as Villas says, 'Gérard's artistic talents extend into regions other than those of dream and esoteric literature'. We seem about to witness a return to Baudelaire's or Heine's view of Nerval as above all an artist, a conscious creator of literary works. One can only welcome such a development, while insisting that the reader of Nerval should remain attentive to the objectives and the motives which Nerval himself was at such pains to specify: and that no account of Nerval can really be satisfactory that does not allow us to include every aspect of his enormously varied, yet essentially unified work.

The influence of a poet who has been regarded in so many radically different ways is naturally difficult to discern. More than most poets, Nerval has been 'all things to all men'. We have seen that in many cases, his readers have found in his work only a reflection of themselves, and in such cases it would be illogical to speak of 'influence' at all. One can find many examples of poets and writers who mention Nerval's name with respect and, more frequently still, with affection: Apollinaire's 'je l'eusse aimé comme un frère' is typical. S. A. Rhodes has listed such 'affinities';[50] but likeness or sympathy do not necessarily imply influence.

We may conveniently (but falsely) divide a poet's work into subject-matter and form, for the purposes of deciding where his influence lies. In Nerval's case, the subject-matter is, as we have seen, as vast and as comprehensive as experience itself; so that it is hardly surprising that he should have struck echoes in other men's hearts. The forms of his poems and prose-writing, on the other hand, are essentially (and consciously) traditional, and apart from the possibility that he restored life to the neglected art of sonnet-writing, he can scarcely be regarded as an innovator in matters of form. He may yet be held to offer something absolutely original; and not surprisingly, we must put together what we have divided, in order to find it: the combination of subjects of transcendent and universal importance with a modest simplicity of form and a restrained manner is rare in modern French literature (though not in English), and it is the effect of this which we recognise as Nerval's characteristic tone. Whether this tone can be said to have influenced later writers is difficult to decide, the more especially as his best work appears to be unique. One cannot, for instance, regard Pierre-Jean Jouve's meditations on themes from Nerval's life and work[51] as being 'influenced' by Nerval; the earlier poet is merely providing the later one with a theme on which to elaborate his own variations, as Handel and Haydn did for Brahms, and Velasquez for Picasso. A less tangible link may be seen in the persistence of the theme of memories of early childhood, not an important element even in Romantic literature (most Romantic poets and novelists seem to have started life as adolescents), but very important in Nerval, as later in Proust, whose paragraphs on *Sylvie* are revealing both of Nerval's methods and of his own.[52]

Nerval is generally held to have exerted an undoubted influence in three further respects: first, by his interest in dreams as a source of knowledge (though to his successors they were more often merely a source of 'poetic' imagery); secondly, by his insistence on the importance of French folk-poetry; and thirdly, in his capacity as a translator of German literature. His earlier translations have not attracted a great deal of notice, since comparatists have been chiefly concerned to show what influence German literature had on Nerval's own work. It seems certain to the present writer that Nerval's *Poésies allemandes* of 1830 had a profound influence on at least one major poet: Victor Hugo, who knew Nerval well at this time. Hugo's *Feuilles d'Automne*, published in 1831, show a marked change of manner when compared to *Les Orientales* or *Odes et Ballades*. There is a greater intimacy, a more direct expression of feeling, and increased preoccupation with human experience; there is a sense of weariness at the impermanence of human affections and the futility of human endeavours in the face of the inexorable passing of time; there is also, for the first time in Hugo's work, a glimpse of eternity, vast and terrifying, beyond the limits of human reason but dangerously accessible to the poet's imagination. All these ideas may be found in the translations in Nerval's *Poésies allemandes*, and especially in the poems of Schiller, together with the very words and images in which Hugo expresses them.[53] Curiously, the tremendous impact which they appear to have made on Hugo is not, at this stage, visible in Nerval's own work; this is probably simply because he had not yet acquired as much experience of life as Hugo.

The translations of Heine's poems, being made by a more mature man, are in themselves more sensitive still than the earlier translations of Goethe and Schiller, and exerted a correspondingly wider influence. These versions are in prose, but prose which has all the force of poetry, subtly rhythmical and harmonious. It was on the strength of these translations that in 1891 Georges Rodenbach credited Nerval with the invention of the *vers libre*.[54] Heine's influence on later French poets is attributed by both L. Betz and F. Hirth to the quality of Nerval's translations.[55] Both of these critics find evidence of a knowledge of Nerval's prose versions of Heine in a number of French poets of the second half of the nineteenth century, and particularly in Verlaine. Some of Verlaine's verses do seem to echo Nerval's translations; but echoes of this sort are not easily demonstrated. What one can distinguish is the characteristic bitter-sweet tone of Heine's lyrics, and his self-destructive irony, which Nerval perfectly understood and captured in his translations. One can hear the same voice in Laforgue, who greatly admired Heine's work. It might be argued that Heine represents the end of Romanticism, its clear-sighted, ruthlessly logical end, and the beginning of a new sensibility; that transition from Romantic to modern is as evident in *Les Chimères*, in *Les Filles du Feu* and in

Aurélia as it is in Heine's work, and though the contact with Heine
must have been decisive in fostering the development of Nerval's
thought, his own suffering and his own insight would surely have
led him in the same direction: the tone of 'Fantaisie' (1832) is
already quite characteristic, as we have seen.

While this new sensibility constitutes an implicit negation of
Romanticism, there is one aspect of Nerval's thought which is
positively Romantic, and that is his belief in the importance of
the imagination. In this respect, although Nerval rejected what
we may call the trappings of early nineteenth-century Romanticism, he was more thoroughly Romantic than most of his
contemporaries. His assertion that 'l'imagination humaine n'a
rien inventé qui ne soit vrai, dans ce monde ou dans les autres'
is to be compared with Keats's remark that 'What the imagination seizes as Beauty must be Truth whether it existed before or
not'.[56] This exalted view of the imagination will be glimpsed
again by Baudelaire, and later by Rimbaud; but Nerval alone,
among the French Romantics of an earlier generation, accords
to imagination the kind of importance it had in the eyes of
Coleridge or Keats. His mentors in this respect were undoubtedly the
German poets, and especially Heine, whose own sources (like those
of Coleridge) are to be found in German Romantic philosophy.
This influence, however, surely served only to confirm, as influences
do, what was already latent in Nerval. His was an essentially
religious nature which must have been very receptive to the
notion that the imagination could transcend the world of the finite.

Again, it is difficult to determine to what extent Nerval was
responsible for fostering this view of the importance of the
imagination, with its attendant high estimate of the value of
poetry, although the Symbolists certainly saw him as an innovator in this respect. It is probably reasonable to suggest that the
example of his literary achievement was more immediately
influential than any work of theoretical aesthetics or philosophy
could have been. Perhaps in the long run Nerval will be seen to
have exerted his profoundest influence in an almost entirely
private way; not stimulating a whole generation as the champions
of aesthetic or moral revolutions do, but constantly inspiring
individual poets to express with equal directness their views of the
moral universe.

AN EVALUATION

Nerval himself was in no doubt about what he looked for when it came to judging other writers: in the work, genuine feeling and simplicity of expression; in the man, integrity, both personal and professional. He was more concerned with human values than with aesthetic theory. He tried for his own part to live up to these ideals, and the degree of his success may be measured by the praises of his contemporaries. It is natural therefore that one should be most immediately impressed, as his contemporaries were, by his candid humanity, by the quality of the man and not only of the poet.

That is not to say that our interest in the man should allow us to forget that he was an artist. Nerval disapproved of the kind of investigator who is anxious above all to unearth all those aspects of a writer's experience which the writer himself has taken pains to master, and if necessary reject, in creating his work of art; he criticises 'Le goût des autobiographies, des mémoires et des confessions ou confidences,—qui, comme une maladie périodique, se rencontre de temps à autre dans notre siècle' ('Les Confidences de Nicolas'; II, 1047). He did however realise that some writers are indivisible from what they write, and that he himself was one of these: 'Je suis du nombre des écrivains dont la vie tient intimement aux ouvrages qui les ont fait connaître' (*Promenades et Souvenirs*; I, 139). His work expresses himself above all; but we must not assume that because Nerval lived in a Romantic age, it does so in a typically 'Romantic' way. Nerval had, as we have seen, none of the 'superiority complex' which he detected with amusement in many of his contemporaries. His sense of humour prevented him from posturing, while his insight showed him how often mere egoism and illusion lay at the bottom of Romantic ideals. In a letter to Janin, for instance, he refers to Romantic love in a way that makes nonsense of all the suggestions that Nerval himself was for very long a victim of that malady; he speaks of Laurent Coster, the hero of his *L'Imagier de Harlem*, and of 'la femme idéale, son rêve, *le rêve éternel du génie dominé par l'amour-propre* et que l'auteur de *Faust* avait symbolisé par Hélène' (I, 1015—the italics are mine). Nerval's self-examination has more in common with Montaigne or Descartes than with Vigny or Chateaubriand. His primary concern is neither confession nor self-dramatisation (it will be remembered that he criticised Mirecourt's biography of him because 'on m'y traite en héros de roman'); he tried rather to analyse his experiences as an example of a human life, offering his findings as a modest contribution to man's insight into human nature and his knowledge of God: 'L'expérience de chacun est le trésor de tous'.

What strikes one most about this endeavour, as it is revealed in the writings, is his persistent courage. In one of his earliest poems there is a remarkably prophetic declaration of faith:[1]

> Mon désir généreux part d'une âme bien née,
> Etre auteur et jeuner, voilà ma destinée!
> Je veux remplir le sort que les dieux m'ont offert,
> Et suivre à l'hopital, Malfilatre et Gilbert.
> Tu ris, mon cher rival, tu plains mon infortune,
> Tu crois que mon esprit est parti dans la lune,
> Que mon glorieux sort fera peu de jaloux,
> Et qu'il faudra me mettre à l'hopital des fous.

Like his own Adoniram, Nerval recognised his destiny and followed it without hesitation; no argument, material or emotional, could deflect him. He was prepared to concede everything to his father but this one immovable ideal. No adversity could shake him from his determination; failure, indifference, misunderstanding, debt, heartbreak and madness merely enriched the subsoil of his art. Men who are prone to melancholy generally try to avoid facing unpleasantness of any kind, for the sufficient reason that their labile emotions too easily turn to sadness. Yet Nerval believed it was his duty faithfully to report the darker side of life; hence his long and steady look at nocturnal Paris: 'Si je n'étais sûr d'accomplir une des missions douloureuses de l'écrivain, je m'arrêterais ici; mais mon ami me dit comme Virgile à Dante:—*Or sie forte ed ardito;—omai si scende per si fatte scale . . .*'— which Nerval translates: 'Sois fort et hardi; on ne descend ici que par de tels escaliers' (*Les Nuits d'Octobre*; I, 94). The same honesty, and the same sense of mission, informs his accounts of his own madness.

His determination is perhaps best expressed in the person of Léo Burckart. Nerval put a great deal of himself into this play, and in his moment of decision Léo Burckart speaks with the voice of the self-effacing poet who had seen the visions of *Aurélia* and was not afraid to say so:[2]

Qui me donnera l'expérience de toutes ces épreuves, ou plutôt la confiance de m'en passer? Ah! si je pensais être autre chose ici qu'un instrument dans les mains de la Providence, j'aurais peur à présent . . . je fuirais comme un lâche avant le combat . . . Mais . . . je n'ai pas le droit de refuser! . . . Si, comme un homme de peu de foi, je recule devant un fantôme . . . qu'aurai-je à dire un jour en paraissant devant le juge éternel, quand des milliers de voix s'élèveront contre moi, criant: Malheur à celui qui pouvait et qui n'a pas osé! Malheur à l'égoïste! malheur à l'infâme! . . . Oh! non, non; Dieu n'a pas mis en moi cette flamme pour que je l'éteigne! Qu'elle me consume, mais qu'elle éclaire! . . .

His courage was, as he meant it to be, exemplary. He had a strong sense of having embarked on a quest which required the utmost in patience, endurance and belief in the value of his actions; not, it must be emphasised, belief in a successful outcome: he might never have succeeded, but he persisted in believing that the effort must be made. For the real value of what he was doing lay not in its chances of success but in its demonstration of human possibilities.

The assertion of human value is nowhere more poignant than in classical tragedy, and the greatness of the tragic hero is often thought to lie in his defiance of destiny even in the face of inevitable defeat; he has, like Nerval's Antéros, 'sur un col flexible une tête indomptée'. Yet for all its nobility, and for all the exaltation which it can and does arouse in the human mind, this defiant heroism has a certain emptiness at its core. It is too unstable to provide a moral basis for living. The impulse towards heroism must be constantly renewed if the exaltation is to be maintained. The hero cannot achieve a once-for-all equilibrium with forces which he sees as bent on his destruction. For this reason, there can be no sense of final achievement, but only of a temporary and precarious respite from a conflict which must, in time, begin again. Nerval has been seen as a tragic hero of this kind, and as a Romantic rebel; but in my view it is one of his particular virtues, given the times in which he lived, that he refused to be blinded by the superficial splendour of Romantic rebellion, and understood that this particular heroic stance, being born of despair and not of hope, was at best a useful expedient in moments of stress. The real solution lay beyond rebellion in the far more difficult achievement of reconciliation: in the acceptance of injustice, danger and defeat with an unfailing love which disarms the power of destiny by *not* assuming that the universe is bent on the destruction of man.

The urgency and the difficulty of this task are clearly expressed in *Aurélia* and in *Les Chimères*, and the slow stages by which the poet came to a full realisation of the nature of his problems can be followed through many of his other works. It is no exaggeration to say that he worked out his salvation through his writing. The tensions in his work are the tensions of his mind, and if the voice sings beautifully, it is as a result of a long discipline in which he learned the difficult nature of harmony.

The value which Nerval himself saw in poetry, and indeed in literature of all kinds, was thus a spiritual value, aesthetic in the highest sense, and nothing to do with the attractions of the surface. Poetry is for him the most complex and the most valuable kind of human utterance, capable both of expressing and of resolving human problems. Time and again, in his critical writings, Nerval makes it clear that in his view, even the highest degree of outward beauty cannot compensate for the lack of something to say to the reader, or for the absence of what he conceives as the proper attitude for a poet, which is one of modest involvement, neither patronising nor aloof. It would evidently be wrong, since he held this view, to try to evaluate Nerval's poems as 'aesthetic objects' unrelated to their creator. We can consider them as objects only in so far as we regard them as concrete expressions of the poet's values. It is meaningless, in any case, to ask if an object is 'beautiful' unless we can first define what we mean by beauty and, if we are to evaluate its creator's achievement, unless we can understand what he himself meant by beauty. Apollinaire, who thought of Nerval as a brother, once defined beauty as 'simplicity', 'grace', and 'goodness'.[3] It is a definition, one feels, to which Nerval would have subscribed. In our own day the moral values he sought in literature are often neglected in favour of purely 'aesthetic' considerations. It is not the least of Nerval's virtues that he persisted in applying moral parameters in a society that was already tending towards a blind materialism, and consequently forcing many of its artists into a position of defiant aestheticism of which we are the heirs.

It may be objected that good intentions do not make a great poet, and that is perfectly true. We cannot judge Nerval's work in any meaningful way if we ignore his intentions; but once we have taken those intentions into account, we are at liberty to ask whether he succeeded in carrying them out, and whether what he actually achieved is of value. In the last analysis, estimates of a poet's value depend very much on the experience and the personal preferences of the reader—and experience, in this context, includes the reader's experience of literature. Compared with the achievements of certain other poets (with, for instance, his contemporary Victor Hugo), the work of Nerval may seem slight, lacking in movement and in breadth of vision. But what it lacks in movement it makes up for in balance, and if its vision is not vast (and that is a debatable point, for there is scarcely an element of heaven or earth which does not implicitly come within his scope), it is certainly intense. His aim was always the concentration and distillation of experience, and he tries deliberately to avoid the disturbance of violent movement, in an effort to catch the moment when opposing forces hold each other in perfect equilibrium. If one regards greatness as dependent on sheer size (and Somerset Maugham once seriously suggested that the human mind is liable to equate the two), then Nerval will not be described as 'a great poet', though he is certainly unique. My own feeling is that his work has greatness of spirit, combined, as he thought it ought to be in the highest genius, with a perfect fitness of expression. In 'Les Confidences de Nicolas' (II, 1048, 1126), Nerval criticises Restif de la Bretone for lacking both 'le sens moral dans sa conduite' and 'l'ordre et le goût dans son imagination', for, he insists, 'le génie n'existe pas plus sans le goût que le caractère sans la moralité'. This association of 'le sens moral' with 'le goût' is revealing; one might see them both as an awareness and a graceful acceptance of necessary limitations. In Nerval's own case, the moral and the poetic genius are certainly inseparable. Both in his life and in his work he shows an intuitive sense of due proportion; his manner is never solemn, though his aims were profoundly serious. In *Aurélia* the moral genius dominates and his method is analytical; though *Aurélia* is certainly unique, Nerval's greatest triumphs as an artist, in my view, are in *Sylvie* and *Les Chimères*, where he goes beyond analysis to achieve a synthesis of experience which has the close-knit texture of contrapuntal music. Nerval attributed to music the power of instilling its harmony into the world; the marvellous passage in the *Mémorables* (I, 410) in which he describes the birth of universal harmony is an allegory of the unifying and reconciling power of art, and of his own art in particular:

Du sein des ténèbres muettes deux notes ont résonné, l'une grave, l'autre aiguë,—et l'orbe éternel s'est mis à tourner aussitôt. Sois bénie, ô première octave qui commenças l'hymne divin! Du dimanche au dimanche enlace tous les jours dans ton réseau magique. Les monts te chantent aux vallées, les sources aux rivières, les rivières aux fleuves, et les fleuves à l'Océan; l'air vibre, et la lumière brise harmonieusement les fleurs naissantes. Un soupir, un frisson d'amour sort du sein gonflé de la terre, et le chœur des astres se déroule dans l'infini; il s'écarte et revient sur lui-même, se resserre et s'épanouit, et sème au loin les germes des créations nouvelles.

From his own darkness, Nerval created a music of this kind, which embraces the accidents of time and space in its 'réseau magique', and affirms the reality of 'Cette chanson d'amour qui toujours recommence'.

X

SOME VIEWS OF GÉRARD DE NERVAL

La Critique doit son origine et sa force à toute décadence artistique et littéraire; les belles époques grecque et romaine ignoraient ce raffinement. A la suite des grands maîtres, sont venus les commentateurs et les panégyristes, comme les parasites et les esclaves derrière un roi . . .

> Nerval, 'Sur la Critique', *L'Artiste*, 1844, Série IV, vol. ii, p. 225. Reprinted in O.C. I, pp. 208–10.

Il importe de remarquer que Nerval est passé dans la catégorie des grands au titre de 'Voyant', et qu'à ce titre, ses sectateurs ont eu tendance à exagérer le caractère 'à part' de son œuvre, de son expérience, de son message . . . Quiconque se soumet à une enquête historique constate: 1° l'unité de la vie et de l'œuvre de Nerval; 2° la parenté de Nerval avec ses contemporains.

> L. Cellier, *Où en sont les recherches sur Gérard de Nerval?*, Archives des Lettres Modernes no. 3, May 1957, p. 21.

(Nerval) has compressed years of experience into a few words, but these words are the quintessence of that experience, not a series of clues to events in his own life.

> J. W. Kneller, 'The Poet and his *Moira*: "El Desdichado" ', *PMLA*, September 1960.

Gérard n'avait à son service qu'un petit bagage. La faculté qu'on appelle *imagination*, ou plutôt *invention*, lui manquait complètement: ou il se perdait dans le pays des chimères, ou il revenait à l'observation de lui-même, qui est un terrain peu fertile, dont un grand esprit comme Montaigne a pu tirer un livre, mais un seul . . .

> Champfleury, *Grandes figures d'hier et d'aujourd'hui*, cited by J. Richer, *Nerval par les témoins de sa vie*, Minard (Nouvelle bibliothèque nervalienne), 1970, p. 193.

C'est un point bien curieux dans la psychologie de la création littéraire chez Nerval que ce manque de souffle, cette impuissance

à créer de son imagination. Sa vie et ses lectures viennent combler
cette lacune . . . il lui faut le détail vécu ou la création livresque
pour que son fonds latent prenne une forme et s'incarne dans un
moule tout fait.

> N. Popa, 'Le Thème et le sentiment de la mort chez Gérard de
> Nerval', *Mélanges de l'Ecole Roumaine en France*, 1925, Pt. 2, p. 68 n. 1.

Nerval oriente ses lectures vers ses préoccupations mystiques
dominantes . . . il cherche des aliments à des obsessions qui
datent de son enfance et qu'il a nourries à des sources livresques
allemandes, scandinaves, françaises, latines et orientales . . .

. . . Nerval lecteur fait un peu figure de victime, d'apprenti
sorcier: seul et désarmé il n'arrive pas à maîtriser les forces
redoutables puisées dans les grimoires et qui se livrent dans sa
cervelle à une diabolique farandole . . .

> J. Richer, *Gérard de Nerval et les Doctrines ésotériques*, Editions du
> Griffon d'Or, 1947, pp. xiv–xv.

Nerval, en composant les sonnets des *Chimères* selon la symbolique
alchimique traditionnelle, suit une méthode de création poétique
qu'on pourrait nommer une méthode d'imagination dirigée. Il
se soumet à l'ordre de succession des couleurs alchimiques: noir-
blanc-rouge, et à l'ordre de succession des divinités hermétiques;
il s'attache à ne faire aucune erreur du point de vue de l'allégorie
alchimique la plus stricte . . . Nerval vise nettement à donner
l'impression—avant la lettre—d'une écriture automatique, d'une
écriture non dirigée, alors qu'il s'agit, tout au contraire, d'une
écriture dirigée très consciemment, d'une imagination qui se fixe
sur les thèmes d'une allégorie traditionnelle découverte dans
Pernety et non pas d'une imagination déroutée . . .

> G. Le Breton, 'La Clé des *Chimères*: L'Alchimie', *Fontaine* no. 44,
> Summer 1945.

(. . .) on ne peut que refuser d'admettre que Nerval ait simplement versifié la description de l'expérience alchimique ou les
secrets du Tarot. La magie du poème reste aussi mystérieuse après
ces commentaires qu'avant; c'est qu'ils n'*expliquent* rien . . .
Ramenons à leur juste proportion les emprunts de Nerval aux
textes ésotériques qu'il ne se borne pas à transcrire; . . . il en fait

exactement le même usage qu'une poésie moins hermétique fait des oiseaux, des arbres et des fleurs.

> A. Béguin, 'Poésie et occultisme', in *Poésie de la Présence*, Editions du Seuil, 1957, p. 141.

Nous sommes persuadés, quant à nous, que Rimbaud, même s'il n'avait pas connu une couple de traités hermétiques . . . n'aurait point révélé au monde des poèmes fondamentalement différents . . .

Des considérations analogues vaudraient pour Nerval, Hugo et Mallarmé: la gnose hermétique a facilité leurs expériences d'alchimie du verbe sans jamais provoquer ces dernières, ni même les fournir d'éléments étrangers.

> A.-M. Schmidt, 'Rimbaldisme, gnosticisme, hermétisme', *La Table Ronde*, November 1949.

Je veux dire que les Chimères ne peuvent s'expliquer par les Tarots . . ., elles ne peuvent pas non plus s'expliquer par cette sombre parturition de principes qui est à la base de la Mythologie, car les principes de la Mythologie furent des êtres dont Gérard de Nerval n'avait pas besoin pour être. (. . .) Ce qui veut dire que loin d'expliquer Gérard de Nerval par ses sources . . . je dirai que l'histoire, la Mythologie et l'alchimie sont venues de ce courant animique interne dont de très rares grands poètes de l'histoire ont manié la puissance d'être . . . Ce qui veut dire que loin de voir expliquer Gérard de Nerval par la Mythologie et l'alchimie, je voudrais voir expliquer l'alchimie et ses Mythes par les poèmes de Gérard de Nerval.

> Antonin Artaud, 'Sur les Chimères' (Letter to Georges Le Breton, dated 7 March 1946), *Tel Quel* no. 22, Summer 1965, pp. 6–7.

Mille détails de doctrine ne font pas la doctrine . . . Pas plus qu'il ne saurait construire un véritable système, l'esprit non systématique de Nerval ne peut comprendre complètement peut-être un système philosophique. Et à la fois aucune des fascinations dont il est la proie n'efface complètement en lui le sens critique.

> M.-J. Durry, *Gérard de Nerval et le Mythe*, Flammarion, 1956, p. 61.

Sauf le cas particulier où le souci du rare a poussé Nerval à exhumer des documents peu connus, il se contente le plus souvent de puiser à tort et à travers dans des ouvrages de vulgarisation . . .

Il est évident que Nerval, comme tout véritable écrivain,
emprunte son bien n'importe où.

> L. Cellier, *Où en sont les recherches sur Gérard de Nerval?*, *Archives des Lettres Modernes* no. 3, May 1957, p. 12.

Il ne faudrait pas croire que la seule lecture de vieux grimoires,
appuyée de dons poétiques singuliers, eût suffi à produire
l'incroyable réussite nervalienne: bien plus étroitement qu'aux
Illuminés du XVIIIe, Nerval se rattache à un large et profond
mouvement qui parcourt son époque. L'œuvre nervalienne met
en cause le mysticisme confus qui, de 1820 à 1850, a animé tant
de penseurs malhabiles et d'artistes sans génie ... On a parlé
souvent de l'hermétisme nervalien: lui-même s'en défend dans
la Dédicace à Dumas, et il a raison. Pour éclairer les œuvres les
plus obscures, il faut, comme dit Aragon, 'retrouver les circonstances'.

> Jean Gaulmier, *Gérard de Nerval et les Filles du Feu*, Nizet, 1956, pp. 11–12.

Il était plus subjectif qu'objectif, s'occupait plus de l'idée que de
l'image.

> Gautier, *Histoire du Romantisme*, Charpentier, 1874, p. 18.

In Gérard's poetry there is no split between image and meaning,
no explanatory matter; the image carries the whole weight.
Gérard's poetic world is a world of symbols, a world in which
sign and object are interchangeable.

> Margaret Gilman, *The Idea of Poetry in France*, Harvard U.P., 1958, p. 231.

A l'art des premiers romantiques qui proposent encore une
image plus ou moins émule du monde, Nerval, dans *Les Chimères*,
substitue ... un art de l'image suggérant une réalité seconde
qu'il a nommée surnaturelle ou supernaturelle. L'image ne
s'immobilise plus dans la représentation ... elle nous achemine
à une réalité impossible à saisir désormais par l'œil ou par
l'oreille ...

> O. Nadal, 'Poétique et Poésie des Chimères', *Mercure de France*, 1–XI–1955.

Par le mystère dont s'entoure sa pensée, par la création d'un

monde où règne une fantaisie presque infinie, par un sens éton-
nant de la nuance s'unissant aux procédés musicaux, par le don de
suggestion de son verbe, Gérard a préparé le symbolisme.

> Jeanine Moulin, Introduction in *Les Chimères*, Textes Littéraires
> Français, Lille-Genève, 1949, p. L.

On comprend pourquoi beaucoup de poètes de la génération
nouvelle ont choisi, avec la sûre divination de la jeunesse, Gérard
de Nerval comme un de leurs plus indéniables précurseurs. Il
fallut qu'une longue suite de rimeurs virtuoses épuisât les
dernières ressources des vieilles prosodies, pour qu'apparussent
les vrais fils de ce lucide artiste qui ... eut la juste perception de
l'Avenir.

> Henri Strentz, *Gérard de Nerval*, Editions de la Nouvelle Revue
> Critique, 1933, p. 81.

Sans doute aurions-nous pu nous emparer du mot SUPER-
NATURALISME, employé par Gérard de Nerval dans la dédicace
des *Filles de Feu* (*sic*). Il semble, en effet, que Nerval posséda à
merveille *l'esprit* dont nous nous réclamons ...

> André Breton, *Manifeste du Surréalisme* (1924); see *Manifestes du
> Surréalisme*, Pauvert, 1962, pp. 38-9.

Un des faits qui m'a toujours le plus particulièrement frappé, est
que Gérard, vivant en plein romantisme, ... a subi peu l'influence de cette école, dans le fond et dans la forme. Il a sacrifié aux
idées allemandes en donnant une traduction de Goethe; il a
paru très enthousiaste d'Henri Heine, mais au fond il eût donné
l'Allemagne et le romantisme pour une page claire et vivante du
XVIIIe siècle ...

> Champfleury, *Grandes figures d'hier et d'aujourd'hui*, cited by J. Richer,
> *Nerval par les témoins de sa vie*, Minard (Nouvelle bibliothèque
> nervalienne), 1970, p. 179.

De tous les personnages qui composent Nerval l'homme de
culture est peut-être le plus vrai et le plus attachant. Gérard fut
le contraire d'un 'génie à l'état sauvage': c'est ce qui le dis-
tinguera toujours d'un Rimbaud ou d'un Lautréamont. Peu de
romantiques donnent autant que lui l'impression d'être fidèles à

un héritage classique, de lire par vocation et par plaisir, de nourrir en toute occasion leur humanisme.

> R. Jean, *Nerval par lui-même*, Ecrivains de Toujours, Editions du Seuil, 1964, p. 85.

Il est impossible de se faire une idée des soins méticuleux qu'il donna à ce qu'il appelait *la toilette générale de l'ouvrage*; quand tout fut terminé, il revit tout, vers par vers, hémistiche par hémistiche. Courbé sur son œuvre, . . . il appliquait à ce contrôle toute sa science de philologue, toutes ses éminentes facultés de puriste, toutes ses délicatesses d'homme de goût par excellence.

> Joseph Méry, *Les Uns et les autres*, Michel Lévy, 1864, p. 192.

Gérard de Nerval qui est assurément un des trois ou quatre plus grands écrivains du XIXe siècle . . . ce grand génie dont presque toutes les œuvres pourraient avoir pour titre celui que j'avais donné d'abord à une des miennes: *Les Intermittences du Cœur*. Elles avaient un autre caractère chez lui, dira-t-on, dû surtout au fait qu'il était fou. Mais, du point de vue de la critique littéraire, on ne peut proprement appeler folie un état qui laisse subsister la perception juste (bien plus qui aiguise et aiguille le sens de la découverte) des rapports les plus importants entre les images, entre les idées. Cette folie n'est presque que le moment où les habituelles rêveries de Gérard de Nerval deviennent ineffables . . . Et il s'essaye à classer et à décrire des rêves alternés.

> Marcel Proust, 'A propos du "style" de Flaubert', in *Chroniques*, Gallimard, 1927, pp. 207, 211 (first published *NRF*, January 1920).

Sa réputation, solidement établie dans le monde les artistes et des gens de lettres, n'avait pas franchi la porte des salons, où longtemps il resta inconnu. Il avait cependant une grande finesse de style et un don d'observation d'une rare subtilité . . .

> M. du Camp, *Souvenirs littéraires*, Hachette, 1882–3, vol. i, p. 420.

C'est à force de regarder les choses intensément que Nerval parvient, sans altérer la réalité, à en dégager tout le potentiel onirique. Et sans doute est-ce pour cela que les visions les plus hallucinatoires que nous propose *Aurélia* gardent un contact étroit avec la réalité, une prodigieuse qualité concrète. Les effets les plus subtils de lumière, de couleur, de mouvement y naissent d'abord de sensations, de perceptions bien réelles.

R. Jean, *Nerval par lui-même*, Ecrivains de Toujours, Editions du Seuil, 1964, p. 119.

La lecture d'*Aurélia* me paraît plus émouvante par la modestie avec laquelle Nerval a confié son destin à son art, par la confiance qu'il a faite à sa profession, et le souci qu'il a eu de préférer au testament ou à la confidence une forme littéraire. *Aurélia* est à mon avis une leçon suprême de poésie. Le poète est celui qui lit sa vie, comme on lit une écriture renversée, dans un miroir, et sait lui donner par cette réflexion qu'est le talent, et la vérité littéraire, un ordre qu'elle n'a pas toujours . . . En amplifiant, en modelant *Aurélia*, Nerval n'a pas désiré autre chose que de bien préciser à la vie qu'il l'avait comprise . . . c'est parce que le talent, parce que la joie du talent, a pris le dessus sur les autres génies qui chevauchaient Nerval, qu'*Aurélia*, loin de présenter l'incohérence et l'équivoque de nos actuelles interprétations du rêve, donne l'impression d'une logique, d'une béatitude, d'un consentement parfaits.

Jean Giraudoux, 'Gérard de Nerval', in *Littérature*, Grasset, 1941, pp. 100–1.

BIBLIOGRAPHY

I. BIBLIOGRAPHICAL WORKS

A. Marie, *Bibliographie des Œuvres de Gérard de Nerval*, Champion, 1926. (Uniform with the Champion edition of the *Œuvres complètes*.)

J. Senelier, *Gérard de Nerval—Essai de bibliographie*, Nizet, 1959.

—, *Bibliographie nervalienne (1960–1967) et compléments antérieurs*, Nizet, 1968. (Senelier's two volumes are an indispensable *instrument de travail*.)

J. Villas, *Gérard de Nerval—A Critical Bibliography, 1900 to 1967*, University of Missouri Press, 1968. (A very useful work. Part I discusses modern trends in the study of Nerval; Part II lists some four hundred items, with a brief résumé of each, and critical comment; there is a subject index.)

Studies of general trends in Nerval criticism will be found in the following works:

L. Cellier, *Où en sont les recherches sur Gérard de Nerval?*, Archives des Lettres Modernes no. 3, 1957. (The final chapter of the same author's *Gérard de Nerval*, listed below, may also be consulted.)

A. Dubruck, *Gérard de Nerval and the German Heritage*, Mouton, The Hague, 1965. (Contains an '*Etat présent*' of Nerval Studies' chiefly concerned with German influences on Nerval, and a bibliography, both of which are useful but incomplete.)

J. Villas, 'Present State of Nerval Studies: 1957 to 1967', *French Review*, November 1967.

II. WORKS BY GÉRARD DE NERVAL

Œuvres, éd. A. Béguin et J. Richer, Bibliothèque de la Pléiade, Gallimard, vol. I (3rd edition), 1960; vol. II, 1956 (2nd edition, 1961).

The Pléiade edition is incomplete. The following editions fill important gaps:

Œuvres Complémentaires de Gérard de Nerval, Nouvelle Bibliothèque nervalienne, Minard *Lettres Modernes*. Textes réunis et présentés par Jean Richer. (In course of publication.)

    I La Vie des Lettres, 1959.

    II La Vie du Théâtre, 1961.

    III *Piquillo, Les Monténégrins* (Théâtre 1), 1965.

    V *L'Imagier de Harlem* (Théâtre 3), 1967.

VI *Le Prince des Sots*, 1960.

VIII *Variétés et Fantaisies*, 1964.

Des Inédits de Gérard de Nerval, éd. Gisèle Marie, Editions Mercure de France, 1939.

Le Carnet de Dolbreuse, Essai de lecture par Jean Richer, Athens, 1967.

Faust et le Second Faust de Goethe, Traduits par Gérard de Nerval, Michel Lévy, 1868.

Les Deux Faust de Goethe, éd. F. Baldensperger, *Œuvres complètes de Gérard de Nerval*, vol. vi, Champion, 1932.

Léo Burckart, in *Sylvie, Suivie de Léo Burckart et d'Aurélia*, Introduction et notes par Henri Clouard, Editions du Rocher, Monaco, 1946.

The following editions, which contain works available in the Pléiade edition or the *Œuvres Complémentaires*, are chiefly interesting for the editors' comments:

Aurélia ou le Rêve et la Vie, éd. Jean Richer, avec la collaboration de F. Constans, M.-L. Belleli, J. W. Kneller, J. Senelier, Minard *Lettres Modernes*, 1965.

Les Chimères et les Cydalises, éd. Rémy de Gourmont, Librairie du Mercure de France, 1897.

Les Chimères. Exégèses de Jeanine Moulin, Textes Littéraires Français, Giard et Droz, Lille, Genève, 1949.

Les Filles du Feu, Les Chimères. Chronologie et préface par Léon Cellier, Garnier-Flammarion, 1965. (Includes *Jemmy*, which is omitted in the Pléiade edition.)

Les Filles du Feu, éd. N. Popa, *Œuvres complètes de Gérard de Nerval*, vols. iv–v, Champion, 1931.

Les Illuminés, éd. Aristide Marie, *Œuvres complètes de Gérard de Nerval*, vol. iii, Champion, 1929.

Notes d'un Amateur de Musique. Avec une Introduction par André Cœuroy, Les Cahiers de Paris, 1926.

Le Rêve et la Vie, éd. Théophile Gautier and Arsène Houssaye, Lecou, 1855. (i.e. *Aurélia*.)

Voyage en Orient. Texte établi et annoté par Gilbert Rouger, Editions Richelieu, 1950.

III. SUGGESTIONS FOR FURTHER READING

The following list offers only a selection of titles, indicating where necessary what aspects of Nerval's work they deal with. Where works of criticism, and especially articles, have been referred to in the text in such a way as to make their content clear, they have not been included here: full references for all works cited in the text will be found in the

Notes. In Chapter X, Some Views of Gérard de Nerval, each quotation is followed by a full reference to the work cited; these references are not repeated here unless some further indication of the book's content is required.

Brief résumés of most of the following items will be found in J. Villas's *Critical Bibliography* listed in Section I above.

(*a*) *General studies*

R.-M. Albérès, *Gérard de Nerval*, Classiques du XIXe siècle, Editions Universitaires, 1955.

A. Barine, *Névrosés*, Hachette, 1898. Reprinted as *Poètes et Névrosés*, 1908. (Studies of Hoffmann, de Quincey, Edgar Allan Poe and Nerval as examples of 'pathologie littéraire'.)

A. Béguin, *Gérard de Nerval*, Librairie Stock, 1936.

L. Cellier, *Gérard de Nerval, l'homme et l'œuvre*, Connaissance des Lettres no. 48, Hatier-Boivin, 1956. (The best available full-scale study; places Nerval firmly in the context of the literature of his time.)

R. Chambers, *Gérard de Nerval et la poétique du voyage*, Corti, 1969. (Not merely an account of Nerval as a traveller, but a perceptive study of the interplay of poetry and reality in Nerval's work.)

M.-J. Durry, *Gérard de Nerval et le Mythe*, Flammarion, 1956. (An exploration of Nerval's tendency to 'mythicise' his experience.)

A. Fairlie, 'An approach to Nerval', in *Studies in Modern French Literature presented to P. Mansell Jones*, Manchester University Press, 1961. (An admirable introduction to Nerval's work; especially concerned with *Les Chimères* and *Sylvie*, but contains important general comment.)

K. Haedens, *Gérard de Nerval ou la Sagesse Romantique*, Grasset, 1939. (One of the first studies to define Nerval's romanticism and distinguish it from that of his contemporaries.)

R. Jean, *Nerval par lui-même*, Editions du Seuil, 1964. (Includes in particular an excellent discussion of *Sylvie* in 'Le temps délivré', pp. 51 ff.)

A. Marie, *Gérard de Nerval, le Poète et l'Homme*, Hachette, 1914 (reprinted 1955). (A pioneering study, still regarded as a standard work on Nerval.)

S. A. Rhodes, *Gérard de Nerval 1808–1855, Poet, Traveller, Dreamer*, Philosophical Library, New York, 1951; Peter Owen Vision Press, London, 1952. (The only full-length biography in English. Anecdotal, and over-emphasises the autobiographical element in Nerval's work.)

J. Richer, *Nerval, Expérience et Création*, Hachette, 1963 (2nd edition, 1970). (J. Richer's thesis; particular emphasis on the formation of myth and the use of esoteric sources; vast, erudite and stimulating.)

— (éd.), *Nerval par les témoins de sa vie*, Nouvelle Bibliothèque nervalienne,

Minard *Lettres Modernes*, 1970. (A collection of contemporary accounts of Nerval; very useful, since many of these are relatively inaccessible.)

L.-H. Sebillotte, *Le Secret de Gérard de Nerval*, Corti, 1948. (A Freudian interpretation.)

A. Symons, 'The Problem of Gérard de Nerval', *Fortnightly Review*, 1898. Reprinted in *The Symbolist Movement in Literature*, Heinemann, 1899— New edition, 1908. (Immensely influential study, both in England and in France; Nerval is seen as a pre-Symbolist poet.)

(b) Studies of particular works

P. Audiat, *L'Aurélia de Gérard de Nerval*, Champion, 1926.

L. Cellier, *de 'Sylvie' à Aurélia: structure close et structure ouverte*, Archives des Lettres Modernes no. 131, 1971.

F. Constans, 'Les sonnets majeures des "Chimères" ', *Revue des Sciences Humaines*, April–June 1967. (Constans has written, since 1934, a number of extremely interesting articles on Nerval, which are unfortunately scattered in various journals. A list, with *résumés*, will be found in J. Villas's *Critical Bibliography*—see Section I above.)

J. Gaulmier, *Gérard de Nerval et les Filles du Feu*, Nizet, 1956.

J. Geninasca, *Une lecture de 'El Desdichado'*, Archives des Lettres Modernes no. 59, 1965.

—, *Analyse structurale des 'Chimères' de Nerval*, La Baconnière, Neuchâtel, 1971. (More structuralist than Nervalian, but illuminating in flashes.)

A. Lebois, *Vers une élucidation des Chimères de Nerval*, Archives des Lettres Modernes no. 1, March 1957.

G. Le Breton, I. 'La clé des *Chimères*: L'Alchimie', *Fontaine*, no. 44, 1945; II. 'L'Alchimie dans *Aurélia*: Les Mémorables', *Fontaine*, no. 45, 1945.

—, 'Le Pythagorisme de Nerval et la source des "Vers dorés" ', *La Tour Saint-Jacques*, 13–14, 1958.

J. Moulin, *Exégèses des Chimères*, Textes Littéraires Français, Giard et Droz, Lille, Genève, 1949.

G. Poulet, *Trois essais de mythologie romantique*, Corti, 1966. (I. ' "Sylvie" et la pensée de Nerval'. First published in *Cahiers du Sud*, no. 209, October 1938.)

M. Proust, *Contre Sainte-Beuve*, Gallimard, 1954. (IX. 'Gérard de Nerval'; concerns *Sylvie*.)

G. Schaeffer, *Le 'Voyage en Orient' de Nerval: étude des structures*, La Baconnière, Neuchâtel, 1967.

(c) Works containing extended discussions of Nerval

F. Alquié, *Le Désir d'Eternité*, Presses Universitaires de France, 1947. (The chapter 'Le Refus affectif du temps' discusses *Sylvie*.)

A. Béguin, *L'Ame romantique et le Rêve*, Editions Cahiers du Sud, Marseille, 1939; (Nouvelle édition), Corti, 1960.

B. Juden, *Traditions Orphiques et Tendances mystiques dans le romantisme française (1800-1855)*, Editions Klincksieck, 1971-.

Ch. Mauron, *Des Métaphores obsédantes au mythe personnel—Introduction à la psycho-critique*, Corti, 1963. (Chapter IV, 'Nerval'; Chapter IX, 'Nerval: Artémis'. Mauron's article 'Nerval et la psycho-critique', *Cahiers du Sud*, no. 293, 1949, is a review of Sebillotte's book listed above; Mauron finds Sebillotte not radical enough.)

G. Poulet, *Etudes sur le temps humain*, Plon, 1950. (On the treatment of time in Nerval's work; cf. Chapter XIV.)

—, *Les Métamorphoses du Cercle*, Plon, 1961. ('Nerval et le cercle onirique', reprinted from *Cahiers du Sud*, no. 331, October 1955.)

J.-P. Richard, *Poésie et Profondeur*, Editions du Seuil, 1955. (Impressionistic studies of Nerval, Baudelaire, Verlaine, Rimbaud; Chapter I, 'Géographie magique de Nerval'.)

(d) Translations containing interesting comments on Nerval

R. Aldington, *Aurelia*, Chatto and Windus, 1933. (An Imagist view, which attempts to detach Nerval from the Romantic movement.)

N. Glass, *Journey to the Orient*, Peter Owen, 1972. (Contains part of 'Les Femmes du Caire', and the episodes concerning Hakem and the Queen of Sheba.)

Vyvyan Holland, *Dreams and Life* [i.e. *Aurélia*], The First Edition Club, Boar's Head Press, 1933. (Sees Nerval as essentially Romantic.)

G. Wagner, *Gérard de Nerval, Selected Writings*, Peter Owen, 1958. (The paperback edition by London Panther, 1968, contains an additional chapter 'Proust on Nerval', a translation by Sylvia Townsend Warner of the pages on Nerval in Proust's *Contre Sainte-Beuve*, listed above.)

James Whitall, *Daughters of Fire*, Heinemann, 1923. (Nerval as a pre-Symbolist.)

Translations of *Les Chimères* have not been notably successful. Andrew Hoyem's *Chimeras* (Dave Haselwood Books: San Francisco, 1966), one of several recent versions, is described as 'Transformations of *Les Chimères*'; despite inaccuracies and idiosyncrasies, the final lines of his 'El Desdichado', which are not a translation at all, but an inspired interpretation, show a poet's insight:

'In the shadow of glorious deeds, of wealth and earthly honor, of special dispensation from the gods, and of a long chain of loves, I rescue from among the list of my accomplishments solely the ability to sing this sad song.'

NOTES

CHAPTER I

1. Glogau, in Silesia, was originally Polish, but was included in the Germanic Confederation after 1815.

2. Eugène de Mirecourt (i.e. C. J. B. Jacquot), *Gérard de Nerval*, Roret, 1854, pp. 17–18.

3. J. P. Eckermann, *Gespräche mit Goethe*, Artemisverlag, Zürich, 1948, p. 383.

4. Cf. Ch. Dédéyan, *Gérard de Nerval et l'Allemagne*, SEDES, 1957–9; A. Dubruck, *Gérard de Nerval and the German Heritage*, Mouton, The Hague, 1965.

5. Letter to Francis Wey (I, 1124). A note in 'Sur un Carnet' (I, 427) more positively states: 'Ce que c'est que les choses déplacées!—On ne me trouve pas fou en Allemagne'.

6. 'I would not yearn so much for Germany, if my mother were not there . . .'; in *Zeitgedichte*, Elsterausgabe I, p. 319. For details of these unpublished notes, formerly in the Marsan collection, I am indebted to Mlle Gisèle Marie (personal communication).

7. Théophile Gautier, *Histoire du Romantisme*, Charpentier, (2nd ed.), 1874, p. 18.

8. For details of this essay see the section 'Language and Form' in the Introduction to the edition of *Les Chimères*, Athlone Press, 1973 .

9. I, 471. Nerval's poem 'Notre-Dame de Paris' (1832; I, 17) refers to Hugo's novel of that name, 'le livre de Victor' (published in 1831), and gracefully suggests that it will outlive the cathedral itself.

10. See J. Richer, *Nerval, Expérience et Création*, Hachette, 1963, pp. 157–61, and plate Ms.4.

11. Twenty years later we find Nerval writing to his father from Strasbourg: 'Je voudrais bien avoir de tes nouvelles, car, avec tant d'amis, je n'en ai pas que tu reçoives, sinon par hasard' (I, 1119).

12. Gautier, 'Marilhat', *Revue des Deux Mondes*, July 1848.

13. Nerval was a frequent visitor to Hugo's salon at this period, and wrote a dramatic version of Hugo's novel *Han d'Islande* in 1829.

14. *Des Inédits de Gérard de Nerval*, éd. Gisèle Marie, Editions Mercure de France, 1939, p. 99.

15. Cf. *Le Monde Dramatique*, i, 248, 276, ii, 346.

16. Nerval refers to Balzac's similar difficulties in a letter to his father

(I, 1110): 'Il a fini par tout payer, lui; il est mort *honoré* comme le disait son prénom'.

17. See *Notes d'un Amateur de Musique*, éd. André Cœuroy, Les Cahiers de Paris, 1926—a collection of Nerval's writings on music and of his theatre reviews. A more recent collection is edited by Jean Richer (*La Vie du Théâtre*, O.C. II, 1961).

18. *Le Carnet de Dolbreuse*, éd. Jean Richer, Athens, 1967, p. 44.

19. Maxime Du Camp, *Souvenirs littéraires*, ii, Hachette, 1882–3, p. 162. Du Camp's reliability has been questioned by biographers of his friend Flaubert; but his accounts of Nerval are well supported by the poet's own testimony and by that of Gautier, among others.

20. Ibid., p. 166.

21. Ibid.

22. Cf. 'Les Confidences de Nicolas' (II, 1001): 'un sentiment singulier qu'éprouvent tous ceux qui voient de près pour la première fois une femme de théâtre'; 'cette statue adorée descendue de son piédestal'.

23. Cf. Gilbert Rouger, 'Notice', in *Voyage en Orient*, i, Editions Richelieu, 1950, pp. 66–8.

24. First so called by Gautier and Houssaye, who believed that these texts were the letters referred to in *Aurélia*; they are published in the Pléiade edition under the title *Lettres à Jenny Colon* (I, 747–68), although the editors are doubtful about the proposed destination of some of them. For a recent review of the whole problem see J. Senelier, *Un Amour inconnu de Gérard de Nerval*, Minard, 1966.

25. Cf. Léon Cellier, *Où en sont les recherches sur Gérard de Nerval?*, *Archives des Lettres Modernes* no. 3, May 1957.

26. Nerval was nonetheless aware of the dangers of excessive detachment in this context; cf. note 3 to Chapter VII below.

27. Daniel-A. de Graaf, 'Gérard de Nerval traducteur de Henri Heine', *Les Langues Modernes*, March–April 1955.

28. Nerval's translation of *Intermezzo* was published in 1848; see Chapter IV.

29. Du Camp, *Souvenirs littéraires*, ii, p. 162. See, in *L.C.*, commentary on 'Artémis'.

30. Jean Richer, 'Nerval et ses deux Léo Burckart', *Mercure de France*, December 1949.

31. Gautier, *Histoire du Romantisme*, p. 134.

32. Nerval was certainly depressed before his departure for Vienna, and there is evidence of illness in 1836 during a voyage to Holland and Belgium (cf. letter to his father, I, 798: 'Je me souviendrai des fièvres de la Belgique').

33. A. Marie sees it as an apology; cf. Introduction, *Les Illuminés*, Champion, 1929, pp. xi–xii.

34. Nerval's spelling; 'Restif (or Rétif) de la Bretonne' is more common.

35. See Introduction to *L.C.*; and below, Chapter III.

36. S. A. Rhodes, 'Gérard de Nerval's Unfinished Novel', *The Romanic Review*, December 1944.

37. Nerval was much preoccupied with Faust; a fragment of a play, *Nicolas Flamel* (1831; published in O.C. III), also has a Faust-like hero.

38. See commentary on this sonnet in *L.C.*

39. See note 2 above. Nerval saw the biography in the bookshops in Strasbourg.

40. 'Georges Bell' was the pen-name of Joachim Hounau. J. Richer refers to him as 'George Bell', but Nerval always calls him 'Georges'; Méry does likewise in *Les Uns et les autres* (Michel Lévy, 1864, pp. 198–9); and Bell's own study of Nerval is signed 'Georges Bell'.

41. J. Richer proposes convincingly that that part of the text of *Aurélia* which concerns the events of 1841 was actually written at the earlier date, and that in 1853–4 Nerval added to this text and completed it with the account of his experiences in 1853. See *Aurélia*, éd. J. Richer, Minard, 1965.

42. See Dr Blanche's letter to Nerval's cousin (I, 1152) and his letter to the Archbishop of Paris (I, 1169–70).

CHAPTER II

1. Two portraits by Nadar are known to exist (see J. Senelier, *Gérard de Nerval—Essai de Bibliographie*, Nizet, 1959, p. 326).

2. Gautier, *Histoire du Romantisme*, p. 70.

3. In *Grandes Figures d'hier et d'aujourd'hui*, cited by J. Richer, *Nerval par les témoins de sa vie*, Minard, 1970, p. 176.

4. Gautier, *Histoire du Romantisme*, p. 70.

5. Henri Heine, *Poëmes et Légendes*, Calmann-Lévy, 1892, Préface, p. vii. An extract from this preface is reprinted in O.C. I, pp. 91–2.

6. Gautier, *Histoire du Romantisme*, p. 70.

7. Ibid., p. 139.

8. Cf. H. H. Houben, *Gespräche mit Heine*, Rütten u. Loening, Potsdam, (2nd ed.), 1948, pp. 586, 759.

9. Du Camp, *Souvenirs littéraires*, i, p. 420.

10. Gautier, *Histoire du Romantisme*, p. 74. Before adopting the name of Nerval, the poet constantly changed his pen-name when writing in journals. His early volumes were signed 'Gérard', the name by which he was generally known to his contemporaries.

11. Cf. letters to Godefroy (I, 1146, 1148); and *Angélique* (I, 161–3).

12. Cf. Georges Bell, cited by L. Cellier, *Gérard de Nerval*, Hatier-

Boivin, 1956, p. 49 (and see J. Richer, *Nerval par les témoins de sa vie*, p. 46).

13. Du Camp, *Souvenirs littéraires*, ii, p. 160–1.

14. Ernst Kretschmer, *The Psychology of Men of Genius* (trans. Cattell), Kegan Paul, 1931, Chapter VI passim.

15. Georges Benoist, 'Gérard de Nerval et Joseph Méry', *Revue d'Histoire Littéraire de la France*, April 1930.

16. Du Camp, *Souvenirs littéraires*, ii, p. 167.

17. Asselineau, cited by Gauthier-Ferrières, *Gérard de Nerval*, Lemerre, 1906, p. 287.

18. Balzac, *Correspondance avec Zulma Carraud*, Gallimard, 1951, p. 224.

19. Mirecourt, *Gérard de Nerval*, p. 45.

20. See for example G. Rouger, 'Notice', *Voyage en Orient*, pp. 55–63.

21. Ibid., p. 66.

22. Cf. also Nerval's comments on Restif de la Bretone's 'réalisme' (II, 1093).

23. Cf. Nerval's remarks on memoirs and confessions (II, 1090).

24. Kretschmer, op. cit., p. 52.

25. J. Richer, 'Nerval et ses Fantômes', *Mercure de France*, June 1951.

26. Moreover, in a letter to Dumas complaining that Dumas's *Le Mousquetaire* had not printed the whole text of *La Pandora*, Nerval remarks 'vous avez coupé la sirène en deux,—j'apporte la queue' (I, 1161).

CHAPTER III

1. See Introduction to *L.C.*

2. He remarks also that 'Il est difficile de devenir un bon prosateur si l'on n'a pas été poète . . .' ('Sur les Chansons populaires'; I, 461).

3. Direct references to his personal experiences are to be found only in works dating from the last year of his life; see above, Chapter I.

4. A. Marie, *Gérard de Nerval, le poète et l'homme*, Hachette, (2nd ed.) 1955, p. 29. (First published 1914.)

5. G. Marie, *Des Inédits de Gérard de Nerval*, p. 9.

6. Mirecourt, *Gérard de Nerval*, pp. 11–12.

7. 'Les Ecrivains', in G. Marie, *Des Inédits de Gérard de Nerval*, p. 56.

8. 'Epître Seconde', ibid., p. 81. The orthography is Nerval's.

9. J. Tiersot, *La Chanson populaire et les écrivains romantiques*, Librairie Plon, 1931, p. 51. A more recent work by Paul Bénichou, *Nerval et la Chanson folklorique*, Corti, 1970, examines this aspect of Nerval's work in detail.

10. See Introduction to *L.C.*

11. 'De l'Avenir de la tragédie', 1837, reprinted in O.C. I, 140. Cf. a similar remark about Sophocles (O.C. II, 578).

CHAPTER IV

1. Cf. Olga Wester Russell, *Etude historique et critique des Burgraves de Victor Hugo*, Nizet, 1962, p. 16.

2. Cf. E. Eggli, *Schiller et le romantisme français*, Librairie Universitaire J. Gamber, 1927, pp. 305–6.

3. See Introduction to *L.C.* ('Sources').

4. Cf. Ch. Dédéyan, *Gérard de Nerval et l'Allemagne*, ii, pp. 288–9.

5. Barker Fairley, *Heinrich Heine, an Interpretation*, Clarendon Press, Oxford, 1954, Chapter I ('Song within song').

6. Heine, Préface, *Poëmes et Légendes*, p. vii; see extract reprinted in O.C. I, 91–2.

CHAPTER V

1. Cf. I, 1217. Léon Cellier, in G. de Nerval, *Les Filles du Feu, Les Chimères*, Garnier-Flammarion, 1965, suggests that Nerval himself saw a unifying theme in the collection, but stresses nonetheless that the volume is composed of 'textes disparates' (Préface, pp. 12–17).

2. The connection between Naples and Vergil's Hell was well known to Nerval's generation; cf. Saint-Marc Girardin, *Souvenirs de Voyage et d'Etudes* (*Italie*, III—'Voyage aux Enfers de Virgile'), Amyot, 1832.

3. Balkis's other name 'Reine Candace' appears on a manuscript version of 'El Desdichado' beside the verse which speaks of 'le baiser de la reine'. Adoniram describes the queen as 'Déesse adorable et funeste!' (II, 538), echoing the narrator's description of the 'bohémienne' in *Octavie*, 'qui me séduisait et m'effrayait à la fois' (I, 289).

4. J. Gaulmier, *Gérard de Nerval et les Filles du Feu*, Nizet, 1956, pp. 36–7.

5. *Angélique* originally formed part of 'Les Faux Saulniers', published in *Le National*, October-December 1850. Cf. I, 1221, n. 1 to p. 160.

6. That Nerval was speaking of his own feelings here is demonstrated by his attempt in 1853 to purchase the piece of land at Loisy in the Valois, in which his mother's family were buried (see letter to his aunt, Mme A. Labrunie; I, 1065). Cf. also *Promenades et Souvenirs* (I, 141): 'il y a dans l'attachement à la terre beaucoup de l'amour de la famille'.

7. Cf. in the seventh letter of *Angélique* a folk-song, which Nerval quotes at length, about a 'père féroce', whose daughter defies him for the sake of her lover, yet refers to him as 'mon père . . . que j'aime tant!' (I, 195).

8. See Introduction to *L.C.* ('Themes').

9. *Voyage en Orient*, II, 342; cf. *Lettres à Jenny Colon IX* (I, 758): 'j'arrange volontiers ma vie comme un roman'.

10. Nerval is referring to Apuleius's *Golden Ass*; cf. *Octavie* (I, 291):

'les détails du culte (of Isis) et des cérémonies que j'avais lus dans Apulée'.

11. Cf. 'Les Confidences de Nicolas' (II, 999): 'une chimère irréalisable . . . qui s'évanouit dès que l'on veut toucher l'idole'.

12. Cf. *Le Marquis de Fayolle* (1849): 'ces blancs fantômes de la jeunesse' (I, 612).

13. The marriage-game had already appeared in *Le Marquis de Fayolle* (I, 645) and in the fragment sometimes known as the 'lettre à Stadler' (I, 459 and note, p. 1284); and it appears again in *Promenades et Souvenirs* (I, 137).

14. This incident is recounted also in *Angélique* (I, 192–3), where the girl is called Delphine.

15. The vines and roses that festoon the village houses at Loisy are referred to again (I, 252); and the inn at Dammartin is similarly described (I, 272).

16. Cf. a note on the Eluard manuscript of 'El Desdichado', beside the eighth line: 'Jardin du Vatican'. See commentary on this sonnet in *L.C.*

17. The 'fille blonde qui mange des citrons' appears also in the notes known as 'Voyage d'Italie—Panorama' (I, 425).

18. Cf. Brisacier's rejection of suicide: 'je suis un comédien qui a de la religion' (I, 152).

19. Cf. *La Pandora* (I, 354–5); and a similar sensation of choking in a dream recounted in *Les Nuits d'Octobre* (1852; I, 106): 'il respire avec peine'—the 'femme mérinos' in this work has a marked resemblance to the dream-images of Pandora.

20. The narrator in *Octavie* waits for the English girl 'sous une treille'— perhaps another source of the image in 'El Desdichado'.

21. Cf. in *Voyage en Orient*, Nerval's comments on 'une illusion passagère': 'Il te semble, non pas que je suis épris, mais que je crois l'être . . . comme si ce n'était pas la même chose en résultat!' (II, 350). This passage was first published in 1847.

22. Cf. 'Les Acteurs anglais' (1844; O.C. I, 223): 'voir jouer *Hamlet*, c'était perdre une illusion, mais acquérir quelques charmantes impressions réelles. Qui pourrait, poète ou artiste, échanger sans regret l'idéal contre un souvenir?' Cf. also a letter to Gautier from Constantinople: 'c'est l'Egypte que je regrette le plus d'avoir chassé de mon imagination, pour la loger tristement dans mes souvenirs!' (I, 933).

23. The Pléiade edition omits *Jemmy*; *Emilie* appeared for the first time in the third edition (1960)—see I, 1218.

24. For a report of Maquet's comments see I, 1258.

25. L.-H. Sebillotte, *Le Secret de Gérard de Nerval*, Corti, 1948.

26. The text was originally considerably longer, and was published

in *la Phalange* (a Fourierist journal) with the title *le Temple d'Isis, souvenir de Pompéi*; in this form it has a more 'documentary' nature, suited to the interests of *la Phalange*.

27. Cellier, Préface, *Les Filles du Feu*, p. 15.

28. See I, 1218.

29. N. Popa, 'Les sources allemandes de deux "Filles du Feu" : Jemmy et Isis', *Revue de Littérature Comparée*, July–September 1930.

30. Nerval preferred to travel on foot, or by stage-coach for very long distances, and seems to have avoided railways where they existed; cf. his choice of route from Compiègne to Paris: 'la plus courte comme distance et la plus longue comme temps' (*Angélique*; I, 180).

31. Cf. *Voyage en Orient* (II, 312) : 'j'ai toujours été plus disposé à tout croire qu'à tout nier'. For the implications of this conscious acceptance of illusion, see Introduction in *L.C.* ('Themes').

32. Cf. the final sonnet of 'Le Christ aux Oliviers', and *Voyage en Orient* (II, 313), where Venus and Adonis are added to this series.

33. Cf. I, 831, 1026, 1110, 1119, 1134.

CHAPTER VI

1. Cf. I, 1264, note 3 to p. 356. Cf. also A. Lebois, '*Aurélia* ou le chamanisme appliqué' : 'nous n'avons aucun texte de Nerval *fou* sauf—peut-être—les dernières pages de *La Pandora*, où l'incohérence des images est inquiétante' (*Les Lettres Romanes*, 1 August 1969).

2. The Pléiade edition ascribes this text to Nicolas Barnaud (cf. I, 1261); it corresponds more exactly to the text transcribed by F. Misson in his *Voyage en Italie*, La Haye, (4th ed.), 1702. Nerval quotes the Latin text in full, with a translation, in *Le Comte de Saint-Germain* (I, 551); his French version is identical with Misson's.

3. Cf. *Sylvie* (I, 245) : 'Je n'aimais qu'elle, je ne voyais qu'elle,—jusque-là !'

4. Cf. note, I, 1260, and letters to Dumas (I, 1161) and Ulbach (I, 1164).

5. The 'pépins de grenade' are echoed in the description of 'la séduisante Pandora' wearing a 'costume des plus légers, avec un caraco blanc brodé de grenats' (I, 1263).

6. This dream resembles the dream in *Aurélia* of 'des îles entourées de flots lumineux', where the narrator meets an old man of his family, whose message he understands without actually hearing it spoken (I, 367).

7. The phrase describing his flight from the Embassy recurs here: 'je me pris à fuir à toutes jambes' (I, 356).

8. For another confidence trick involving boxes of Nuremberg toys, see *Voyage en Orient* (II, 618–19).

CHAPTER VII

1. Cf. *Petits Châteaux de Bohême* (I, 75): 'Une longue histoire . . . et qui ressemble à tant d'autres!'; and *Sylvie* (I, 269–70): 'Que dire maintenant qui ne soit l'histoire de tant d'autres?'

2. The absence of the yardsticks of time and space is characteristic of the dream-world; Heine speaks of this phenomenon, and similarly compares it to our notions of life after death, in his *Reisebilder* (*Schnabelewopski*; in the French edition, *Tableaux de Voyage*, Renduel, 1834, this passage is on pp. 347–8).

3. Cf. *Voyage en Orient* (II, 61); and similar comments on the effect of fiction on real life in the Brisacier episode (I, 150) and in *Sylvie* (I, 266).

4. See their introduction to *Le Rêve et la Vie*, Lecou, 1855, published in the year of Nerval's death; and cf. I, 1275, n. 1 to p. 414. Georges Bell also refers to *Aurélia* as 'Sa dernière œuvre, qui restera inachevée . . .' (*Gérard de Nerval*, Etudes contemporaines, Lecou, 1855, p. 44); and Charles Asselineau, who saw in the first part of *Aurélia* 'un plan mûrement conçu, les intentions les plus littéraires', thought the second part unfinished, but pointing to a return to religion ('Le dernier livre de Gérard de Nerval: Aurélia, ou le Rêve et la Vie', *L'Athenæum Français*, 27 October 1855).

5. Survival in the memory of others is a recurrent theme in Nerval's work; see commentary on 'Horus' in *L.C.* and below, n. 25.

6. Nerval is comparing 'what men call reason' with a 'logic' ('raisonnement') of his own; the same distinction is made in the letter written to Mme Dumas after his illness in 1841 (cf. I, 904), in his discussion of *Hamlet* ('Les Acteurs anglais'; O.C. I, 223), and in 'Le Roi de Bicêtre' (II, 939–54).

7. L. Cellier lists these textual 'rappels' and 'reprises' in *de 'Sylvie' à Aurélia*, Archives des Lettres Modernes no. 131, 1971; his object being to show that *Aurélia* is 'une œuvre initiatique', his interpretation of these patterns differs from mine.

8. For external evidence of these, see Chapter II above.

9. Staircases and corridors reappear in *Les Nuits d'Octobre* (I, 104).

10. Nerval likens the winged figure to Dürer's 'Melancholia', an image that haunted him; see Introduction to *L.C.*

11. See commentary on *La Pandora*, above.

12. The combination of loving affection and justice is what Nerval most missed in his childhood; see commentary on *Isis*, above.

13. The images in this section owe something to Heine's poem 'Frieden' (*Die Nordsee*) which Nerval translated ('La Paix').

14. Cf. letter to Mme Dumas (1841), in which Nerval expresses a similar faith: 'Il me sera resté du moins la conviction de la vie future et de la sympathie immortelle des esprits qui se sont choisis ici-bas' (I, 905).

15. A reference to this dream (sometimes misinterpreted as being a description of dreams in general) occurs in the 'Notes Manuscrites' (I, 421): 'Rêve habit tissé par les fées et d'une délicieuse odeur'.

16. Cf. letter to Antony Deschamps after Nerval's departure from the clinic in 1854: 'Je n'ai plus à accuser que moi-même et mon impatience qui m'a fait exclure du *paradis*' (I, 1158). The security of this enclosed place undoubtedly appealed to him; he was similarly reluctant to leave Sainte-Pélagie prison after his short stay there in 1832: 'La prison m'était devenue si agréable, que je demandai à rester jusqu'au lendemain' (*Mes Prisons*; I, 58).

17. Nerval mentions this accident in letters written in September 1851 (I, 1006–8).

18. This explanation is repeated (I, 385).

19. See commentary on this sonnet in *L.C.*

20. This scene recalls the marriage-scene in the story of Calife Hakem (*Voyage en Orient*; II, 392–4); Hakem also feels that the usurper is his brother and double.

21. The magic sign is probably the mystic Tau which Adoniram uses to summon the degrees of masons in *Voyage en Orient* (II, 536).

22. Cf. Nerval's footnote to the passage of *Aurélia* in which he discusses the mystical unity of the family: 'Je frémis d'aller plus loin, car dans la Trinité réside encore un mystère redoutable' (I, 369).

23. Cf. 'Paradoxe et Vérite' (I, 431): 'Philosophie! ta lumière, comme celle des enfers de Milton, ne sert qu'à rendre les ténèbres visibles'; and see Introduction to *L.C.*

24. This notion is also discussed in *Isis*—see commentary above.

25. That belief in God maintains the existence of God is also suggested in 'Le Christ aux Oliviers'; see also in *Voyage en Orient* (II, 87), a passage about the cults of the ancient gods.

26. A note in 'Sur un Carnet' (I, 426) is tragically aware of the problems of repentance: 'si l'on vous met en état de fièvre, de folie? Si l'on vous bouche les portes de la rédemption?'

27. This movement towards his family is very marked at the end of Nerval's life, when he tried to re-establish relations with cousins he had not met for many years (see letters to Dr Evariste Labrunie, Dublanc and Gautié d'Agen, November 1853, I, 1079–81); he also tried, despite his financial difficulties, to purchase the plot of land in which members

of his mother's family were buried (see letter to his aunt, October 1853,
I, 1065).

28. This phrase seems to refer obliquely to a kind of poetical religi-
osity common in early nineteenth-century Romanticism; Nerval may
be thinking particularly of Chateaubriand's *Le Génie du Christianisme*
(1802), in which Chateaubriand sets out to demonstrate 'la beauté de
cette religion . . . la grandeur de Dieu', referring, in the *Lettre à M. de
Fontanes*, to 'mon livre futur sur les beautés de la religion chrétienne'
(*Le Génie du Christianisme*, Furne, 1865, pp. xx, xxv). It is clear from the
context in *Aurélia* that Nerval regarded this kind of religious thinking
as an inadequate basis for moral decisions.

29. See commentary on 'Le Christ aux Oliviers' in *L.C.*

30. Probably the poet Heine—some corroboration of this account
appears in Houben, *Gespräche mit Heine*, p. 788.

31. This passage recalls 'Vers Dorés', as well as prefiguring Baudelaire's sonnet, 'Correspondances'; see commentary on 'Vers Dorés'
in *L.C.*

32. Cf. I, 359: 'Swedenborg appelait ces visions *Memorabilia*'; the title
Memorabilia (Le rêve) appears also on a manuscript of *La Pandora* (cf.
I, 1265).

33. For the significance of Thor as an image of Nerval's father, see
commentary on *La Reine des Poissons*, above, Chapter II.

34. The parallels between these two passages are striking, and surely
dispose of the idea that *Aurélia* is an unfinished work; Nerval seems on
the contrary to be consciously echoing the beginning of the text to
underline the fact that he has reached the point which he set out to find
and is ready for the final revelation: in the first paragraph, we find the
phrases 'ces portes d'ivoire et de corne', 'cette *Vita Nuova*', 'l'image de
la mort', 'le monde des Esprits', 'un engourdissement' followed by the
continuance of 'l'œuvre de l'existence'; in the later passage, 'ces portes
mystiques', 'une vie nouvelle . . . pareille sans doute à celle qui nous
attend après la mort', 'ces esprits des nuits', 'un engourdissement de
quelques minutes' followed by a new life, linked with waking life ('un
lien entre ces deux existences'; I, 412).

35. Unrequited love was the special concern of Antéros: see commentary on the sonnet of that name in *L.C.*

36. Nerval's letters to Blanche from June 1854 until the end of his
life show his emotional dependence on his doctor, who seems to have
occupied at this time the place which Nerval's father had refused. Despite
the occasional irritations which such dependence was bound to cause,
Nerval consistently acknowledges the younger man's sympathy and
understanding.

CHAPTER VIII

1. Mirecourt, *Gérard de Nerval*, especially pp. 6-7, 33.

2. Letter to his father (I, 1122); Nerval also comments on Mirecourt's book in a letter to Georges Bell (I, 1116).

3. Baudelaire, *L'Art romantique*, Conard, 1925, p. 341. It may be indicative of a general lack of interest in Nerval at this period that Baudelaire mentions him only incidentally.

4. P. Quennell, 'Gérard de Nerval', in *Baudelaire and the Symbolists*, Chatto and Windus, 1927, pp. 66-98. It is only fair to add that the revised edition of this book (1954) offers a much softened version of this condemnation, though Nerval is still described as 'a diligent and successful hireling'.

5. Heine, *Poëmes et Légendes*, Préface, vi-vii. Partly reprinted in O.C. I, p. 91, n. 4.

6. Introduction, *Le Rêve et la Vie*, pp. 28-9.

7. 'Gérard de Nerval', *L'Athenæum Français*, 3 February 1855. This unsigned article may be the work of Nerval's friend Charles Asselineau (cf. above, Ch. VII note 4).

8. Gautier, *Histoire du Romantisme*, pp. 18, 134-6, 150.

9. Champfleury, *Grandes Figures d'hier et d'aujourd'hui*, Poulet-Malassis, 1861; A. Houssaye, *Confessions, souvenirs d'un demi-siècle*, Dentu, 1891. Houssaye is actually quoted as a source in A. Whitridge, 'A Backwater of Romanticism', *North American Review*, 1923. The title of this article in itself suggests that Nerval is being noticed primarily for his quaintness.

10. A. Lang, 'Three Poets of French Bohemia', *The Dark Blue*, May 1871. (Reprinted in *The Bibelot*, vol. 14, 1908).

11. Saintsbury, *Primer of French Literature*, Oxford, 1925, (first published 1880), p. 122.

12. Saintsbury, *A Short History of French Literature*, Oxford, 1917, (first published 1882), p. 525. The comment on the verse is quoted (with slight inaccuracy) from Andrew Lang; in his later *History of the French Novel*, Macmillan, 1917-19, Saintsbury acknowledges the source (ii, p. 256).

13. Saintsbury, *A History of the French Novel*, ii, pp. vi, 255.

14. G. Servières, *Richard Wagner jugé en France*, Henry du Parc, 1887, p. 21.

15. An accident the more ironical if we accept, as seems reasonable, the hypothesis that Nerval did not actually hear *Lohengrin* on the occasion which he describes (II, 795-7), and was helped by his friend Liszt in the writing of his 'review'. See O. Weise, *Gérard de Nerval, Romantik und Symbolismus*, Akademischer Verlag, Halle, 1936, pp. 78-82.

16. G. Kahn, 'Gérard de Nerval', *Revue Indépendante*, November 1888.

17. R. de Gourmont, *Les Chimères et les Cydalises*, Mercure de France, 1897, Préface, pp. 20–2.

18. H. de Régnier, 'Compte-Rendu', *Mercure de France*, 1–xi–1897.

19. James Whitall, in the preface to his translation of *Les Filles du Feu* (*Daughters of Fire*, Heinemann, 1923), states that Nerval was 'the first to discover the symbolical use of language', which seems to imply that Whitall, unlike Symons, thought that Nerval was well aware of what he was doing. (For a list of English translations of Nerval, see Bibliography, Section IV).

20. A. Symons, 'The Problem of Gérard de Nerval', *Fortnightly Review*, 1898. (Reprinted in *The Symbolist Movement in Literature*, Heinemann, 1899; revised edition, 1908.)

21. Dumas had just published 'El Desdichado' with an introduction hinting that Nerval was insane. See commentary on this sonnet in *L.C.*

22. See discussion of the use of these terms (and Baudelaire's 'surnaturaliste') in Introduction to *L.C.* ('Sources' and note 27).

23. S. A. Rhodes, 'Poetical Affiliations of Gérard de Nerval', *Publications of the Modern Language Association of America*, December 1938.

24. A. Balakian, *The Literary Origins of Surrealism*, King's Crown Press, New York, 1947, pp. 37 ff.

25. A. Béguin, *L'Ame romantique et le rêve*, Editions Cahiers du Sud, Marseille, 1939, p. 388 (Nouvelle édition, Corti, 1960).

26. For further discussion of this point, see the section on 'Language and Form' in *L.C.* André Breton is an honourable exception to the rule; for his perceptive views, see commentary on 'Vers Dorés' in the same volume.

27. E. Faguet, 'Gérard de Nerval', *La Revue des Revues*, 1 December 1906. Gauthier-Ferrières's book, described by Faguet as 'une biographie qui peut passer pour définitive', is now out-dated. The reputation of Faguet himself is at a very low ebb; his assessment of Nerval lacks imagination but has at least the merit of observing that Nerval's mysterious effects are obtained by 'des mots *précis* et des images *nettes*'.

28. A. Marie, *Gérard de Nerval, le poète et l'homme*, p. 54.

29. Ibid., pp. 220–1.

30. F. Carco, *Gérard de Nerval*, Albin Michel, 1953; R. Bizet, *La Double Vie de Gérard de Nerval*, Plon, 1928; H. Clouard, *La Destinée Tragique de Gérard de Nerval*, Grasset, 1929.

31. A. Coléno, *Les Portes d'ivoire* (*Nerval-Baudelaire-Rimbaud-Mallarmé*), Plon, 1948.

32. R. Lalou, *Vers une Alchimie lyrique*, Les Arts et le Livre, 1927, p. 61.

33. E. Wilson, 'The Sanctity of Baudelaire', in *Classics and Commercials*, W. H. Allen, 1951, p. 422.

34. A. Coléno, *Les Portes d'ivoire*, p. 27.

35. A. J. Leventhal, 'Gérard de Nerval, Poet and Schizophrenic', *Dublin Magazine*, October–December 1941.

36. Nerval condemns, in the last pages of 'Les Confidences de Nicolas' (II, 1125–6), the fascination with morbidity and disease which he saw in 'cette école si nombreuse aujourd'hui d'observateurs et d'analystes en sous-ordre qui n'étudient l'esprit humain que par ses côtés infimes ou souffrants'.

37. L.-H. Sebillotte, *Le Secret de Gérard de Nerval*, Corti, 1948.

38. G. Michaud, *Message poétique du Symbolisme*, Nizet, 1947, i, p. 33.

39. Béguin, *L'Ame romantique et le rêve*, p. 367.

40. Y.-G. Le Dantec (éd.), *Les Chimères*, Librairie de Médicis, 1947, p. 22.

41. J. Richer, 'Le Luth constellé de Nerval', *Cahiers du Sud*, no. 331, October 1955. M. Richer remarks, having demonstrated the rôle of Nerval's horoscope in 'El Desdichado': 'La merveille, c'est qu'un poème aussi magnifique, dépourvu de sens apparent, ait pu être très consciemment fabriqué par un "fou" malicieux qui avait *sans doute* sous les yeux la figure que nous avons établie à notre tour' (my italics). A similar method is used by M. Richer's more recent note on 'Artémis': 'Sainte napolitaine et sainte de l'abîme', in 'Notes conjointes sur *Artémis* de Gérard de Nerval', *Studi Francesi*, January–April 1970. See also *Vivante étoile*, by J. Richer and O. Encrenaz, *Archives des Lettres Modernes* no. 127, 1971, for arithmosophical variations on Michelangelo, Nerval and André Breton; and J. Richer, *Nerval au royaume des archétypes*, *Archives des Lettres Modernes* no. 130, 1971, on *Octavie*, *Sylvie* and *Aurélia*.

42. A. Béguin, *Gérard de Nerval*, Stock, 1936, p. 92; E. Aunos, *Gérard de Nerval et ses énigmes*, Vidal, 1956, p. 65.

43. H. Bremond, *La Poésie pure*, Grasset, (rev. ed.), 1926, p. 19.

44. Y.-G. Le Dantec (éd.), *Les Chimères*, p. 21.

45. G. Rouger, 'En marge des Chimères', *Cahiers du Sud*, no. 292, December 1948. Nerval's conversation seems sometimes to have produced the same effect; Georges Bell remarks that 'Il avait dans la voix des inflexions si douces qu'on se prenait à l'écouter comme on écoute un chant' (*Gérard de Nerval*, p. 12).

46. A. Lebois, *Vers une élucidation des Chimères*, *Archives des Lettres Modernes* no. 1, March 1957.

47. Alison Fairlie, 'An Approach to Nerval', in *Studies in Modern French Literature presented to P. Mansell Jones*, Manchester University Press, 1961, p. 89.

48. J. Villas, 'Present State of Nerval Studies: 1957 to 1967', *French Review*, November 1967.

49. R. Jean, 'Encore Nerval', *Cahiers du Sud*, no. 349, January 1959.

50. S. A. Rhodes, 'Poetical Affiliations of Gérard de Nerval', *PMLA*, December 1938.

51. P.-J. Jouve, 'Treizième', *La Vierge de Paris*, Egloff, 1945, pp. 225–6.

52. Marcel Proust, 'A propos du "style" de Flaubert', *Chroniques*, Gallimard, 1927, pp. 210–1; cf. also 'Sur Nerval', *NRF*, December 1953, reprinted in *Contre Sainte-Beuve*, Gallimard, 1954.

53. Cf. N. Rinsler, 'Victor Hugo and the *Poésies allemandes* of Gérard de Nerval', *Revue de Littérature comparée*, July–September 1965.

54. G. Rodenbach, 'La Poésie nouvelle', *Revue politique et littéraire (Revue bleue)*, 1891.

55. L. Betz, *Heinrich Heine in Frankreich*, Müller, Zürich, 1895, p. 200; Fr. Hirth, *Heinrich Heine und seine französischen Freunde*, Florian Kupferberg, Mainz, 1949, p. 110.

56. John Keats, Letter to B. Bailey, 22 November 1817.

CHAPTER IX

1. 'Epître Première', *Des Inédits de Gérard de Nerval*, pp. 43–4. The orthography is Nerval's.

2. *Léo Burckart*, éd. H. Clouard, Editions du Rocher, Monaco, 1946, Première Journée, xi, p. 159.

3. Apollinaire, 'Chant de l'Honneur', in *Calligrammes*: 'Mais ici comme ailleurs je le sais la beauté/N'est la plupart du temps que la simplicité . . . Elle porte cent noms dans la langue française/Grâce Vertu Courage Honneur et ce n'est là/Que la même Beauté'

INDEX OF NAMES

Authors of quotations in Chapter X are included only if they appear elsewhere in the text.

INDEX OF CHARACTERS AND WORKS

This Index is intended to help the reader to find comments on important works which do not appear in the list of Contents.